IMMENSE
POSSIBILITIES

IMMENSE POSSIBILITIES

By

Cecelia Frances Page

iUniverse, Inc.
New York   Bloomington

IMMENSE POSSIBILITIES

The views expressed in this work are solely those of the author and do not necessarily reflect the views of the publisher, and the publisher hereby disclaims any responsibility for them.

iUniverse books may be ordered through booksellers or by contacting:

iUniverse
1663 Liberty Drive
Bloomington, IN 47403
www.iuniverse.com
1-800-Authors (1-800-288-4677)

Because of the dynamic nature of the Internet, any Web addresses or links contained in this book may have changed since publication and may no longer be valid.

ISBN: 978-1-4401-7937-2 (sc)
ISBN: 978-1-4401-7936-5 (ebk)

Printed in the United States of America

iUniverse rev. date: 10/21/2009

CONTENTS

PREFACE

IMMENSE POSSIBILITIES

IMMENSE POSSIBILITIES is a stimulating book of 67 stories and articles.

<u>Scientific Topics are:</u> Journey Inside The Earth, The Moon Today And The Future, The Moon Today And The Future, Garden Solariums, Fascinating Minerals and Gems, Changing Weather and Flowers Grow In Unusual Places.

<u>Travel topics</u> are: Beautiful Australia, Mexico's Enchantment, The Summer Place, Survival In the Wilderness and Iceland Wonderland.

<u>Social Topics</u> are: Tremendous Memories, Women and Men's Fashions, Teenage Behavior, Private Moments, Movie Stars Disillusion Us, School Day Experiences, City Life, Happy Times, Ursula's Life In Brookfield, Afraid Of The Dark, Express Yourself, Children Imitate Their Parents, The Will To Live,

Dining Out, How To Be Liked By Others, Glamour Isn't That Important, A Normal Life, New Beginnings and Sparkling Personalities.

Philosophical Topics are: Miracles Work, Phenomenal Changes, Reincarnation, The Seven Fold Path, The Golden Age, Awaken To God, Seek Peace Of Mind and Know Thyself.

Career Topics are: College Seminars, Librarians Succeed, Lawyers Appeal Cases, Maintaining A Car, Policemen Can Be Unfair, Becoming A Well Known Writer and How To Become A Famous Painter.

Psychological Topics are: Raising A Gifted Child, Forgiving Enemies, Kidnapped, Overcoming Grief, Paranoia Revealed and Shocking News.

Other Topics are: Architectural Wonders, Presenting A Speech, Skin Care And Makeup, Using Different Maps, What Is Beautiful?, Cleaning House, Panoramic Visions, Modern Homes, Madonna Inn, Swimming In A Public Pool, American Propaganda, Viet Nam Tragedy, Wearing Glasses, Panda Express Delights and Finger Prints Tell.

You will enjoy reading about many worthwhile topics in this book to expand your awareness.

ABOUT THE AUTHOR

Cecelia Frances Page has been writing poetry, short stories and research papers since the age of 19. Cecelia has a B.A. and M.A. in Education. She also focused in English, Speech Drama and Psychology. Cecelia has published five screenplays and three, original, poetry books. Cecelia is an educator, writer, pianist, vocal soloist, piano and vocal teacher, philosopher, photographer and artist. Cecelia has written 50 books. The name of her books published by iUniverse Publishers are: *Westward Pursuits, Opportune Time, Imagine If...., Power Of Creative And Worthwhile Living, Fortunately, Certain People Make A Difference, New Perspectives, Celestial Connections, Celestial Beings From Outer Space, Awesome Episodes, Vivid Memories Of Halcyon, Phenomenal Experiences, Expand Your Awareness, Adventures On Ancient Continents, Awaken To Spiritual Illumination, Seek Enlightenment Within, Brilliant Candor, Fascinating Topics, Very Worthwhile Endeavors And Circumstances, Horizons Beyond, Pathways To Spiritual Realization, Mystical Realities,*

Magnificent Celestial Journeys, Extraordinary Encounters, Incredible Times, Tremendous Moments, Amazing Stories And Articles, Adventurous Experiences, Extraterrestrial Civilizations On Earth, Relevant Interests, Impressionable Occurrences, Interpretations Of Life, Tangible Realities, Remarkable World Travels, The Future Age Beyond The New Age Movement, Infinite Opportunities, Immense Possibilities, Random Selections and more.

Cecelia Frances Page continues to write books to inspire others and to encourage her readers to be creative, productive human beings. You can order any of these books at www.iuniverse.com. or call 1-800-288-4677, Extension 5454 to order anyone of these books.

ONE

TREMENDOUS MEMORIES

Tremendous memories occur in our lives. Special occasions, events and experiences uplift us. We can recall special moments and happenings to remind us of the good times in our lives.

Sally Fetterson reminisced about the special moments and worthwhile experiences during her life. She was 95 years old. As she sat in her rocking chair she began to remember some of her special memories.

A flashback of a wonderful vacation came into Sally's memory. She recalled camping near Mount Shasta in Northern California. It had rained that morning. A magnificent rainbow reflected a luminous rainbow of colors: purple, pink, yellow, green, orange and blue across the sky in the bright, misty air.

Sally had gone camping with her older brother, Harry, who was also an outdoor person. Sally was 17 and Harry was 19. Both were athletic. Sally remembered climbing Mount Shasta with her brother. He was strong and healthy. Sally admired her brother's abilities.

When Sally and Harry reached the summit of Mount Shasta they saw Shasta Valley below with its lush, verdant grasses and pine trees. They stood on a slope and gazed at the beautiful view, which stretched out for miles. The view was very clear and vivid to behold.

Sally suddenly saw some tall, slender men dressed in white robes. They were barefoot. They had long, blonde hair and they were Caucasians. These group of seven men appeared unexpectedly out of the mist. Sally was surprised to see the spiritual looking beings.

The seven, spiritual men approached Sally and Harry. They were open and friendly to Sally and Harry. Sally, who was nervous at first to meet these unusual beings, began to relax because she felt their higher vibrations and harmonious mannerisms. The men greeted Sally and Harry. "Welcome to our mountain. May we help you?" said one of the men. Another man said, "Don't be afraid. We will not harm you. We live in peace."

Sally finally said, "Hello. Who are you?" The first Shasta man replied, "We live here on Mount Shasta. We have lived here for thousands of years. "Sally asked, "Where do you live on this mountain?" The second man answered, "We live inside Mount Shasta. We are protected inside this mountain." Sally was still amazed at finding out about these spiritual men.

Sally, who was sitting in her rocking chair at the present time thinking about her unusual experience when she was age seventeen at the time thought about this. She continued to think about this experience. She remembered more details about this incident. Sally asked the Shasta men, "Can we see where you live inside of Mount Shasta?" The first man said, "If you can keep our living space a secret, we will show you where we live." Sally and Harry promised to keep it a secret.

The seven men started walking through a tunnel into Mount Shasta. Sally and Harry followed them through a crystal tunnel, which looked transparent. The seven Shasta men, Sally and Harry continued walking through this lit up tunnel.

Finally, everyone came to a large room inside Mount Shasta. This room was glowing with light. There were more Shasta people living within this very large room. They had modern furniture, computers and other facilities inside this enormous, inside, mountain retreat. Outdoor, tropical plants were growing there.

Sally and Harry were greeted by more Shasta people. The Shasta people were all dressed in white or purple robes. They all were barefoot. They were all spiritual looking. Sally and Harry felt comfortable around these advanced people. They were amazed that they could live inside a mountain. Sally and Harry found out that these Shasta people were descendents of the ancient Lemurians. They had lived inside Mount Shasta for thousands of years.

Sally had been sitting in her rocking chair for a while as she recalled her special experience at age 17. She decided to get up and go outside into her garden.

She observed her beautiful flowers and fruit trees spread out in her two acre yard. She felt at peace as she walked around and smelled the pleasant fragrances in her garden.

Sally would never forget her tremendous experience at Mount Shasta. She was glad she had met the Shasta people, who lived in peace inside Mount Shasta.

TWO

JOURNEY TO THE CENTER OF THE EARTH

A journey to the center of the Earth can be a challenging, yet marvelous undertaking. A book authored by Jules Vern's, <u>Journey To The Center Of The Earth</u> was written many years ago. In it he described an expedition of men and a woman who explored the Earth's interior.

Jerry Hanson was an explorer-scientist, who decided to explore the Earth's, interior. He had completed college and had a B.S. degree in Science. Jerry was interested in discovering more about the interior of the Earth.

Jerry Hanson planned an expedition. He invited several co-explorers to go with him to explore the interior of the Earth. Walter Hughes and Sylvester Wilson decided to go exploring with Jerry. The three men packed their gear. They wore hiking clothes and carried climbing equipment and cameras.

Jerry, Walter and Sylvester began their brave, challenging expedition early one morning in August 2010. They were well equipped to go exploring. They brought climbing, spiked boots, ropes, mountain hammers, shovels, long, thick, anchor nails, rope anchors and bedrolls. They also brought canned food packed in their backpacks. Cameras and flashlights were also packed.

Jerry and his followers drove to the Grand Canyon in Arizona. They hiked into the Grand Canyon. They walked deep into this canyon until they came to a place where they found an opening in the Earth. Jerry was pleased to discover this deep opening in the Earth. He discovered a continuous opening in the Earth.

The three expeditioners began walking down a deep hole in the ground. They used their flashlight to light their way as they went deeper and deeper inside the Earth. As they climbed down this deep hole they had to place their feet on ledges carefully. The soil inside the Earth appeared reddish-brown. As they climbed further down the deep hole they used ropes and anchored their way down the hole.

This deep hole went for several miles down into the Earth. Jerry, Walter and Sylvester finally came to the end of the hole. They could look up and see the light in the sky. They landed on rocks at the bottom of the hole. They used their flashlights to look around.

There were caverns at the bottom of this hole. Jerry, Walter and Sylvester decided to explore the caverns. They came across precious gems such as gypsum, opals, rhinestones, jade and even some gold. Jerry was excited. He said, "We should gather these precious gems and stones. They look very valuable." So, Jerry, Walter and Sylvester gathered different gems and stones and placed them into cloth sacks.

It was colder deep in the Earth. Jerry, Walter and Sylvester put on warm jackets to keep warmer. They continued to explore the caverns. They saw snakes slithering across rocks. They were surprised that snakes could live so deep in the Earth.

Jerry decided to take photographs of the snakes. There were brown and green snakes moving around everywhere. Walter and Sylvester took out their cameras and took photographs, too. The three men continued to explore more. They encountered stalactites were long and some dripped to the ground below.

The three explorers walked through the many caverns. They had to be careful of the snakes crawling around in the rocks and pathways. They became tired after walking for some time in the caverns. So they sat on some rocks in order to rest. They were hungry. It was time to eat some of their packed food.

Jerry took out a can of tuna. He opened the tuna and spread it on slices of bread with mayonnaise and mustard and pickles. He also had some potato chips and a cold, ice mango tea in a can. Jerry was very hungry after exploring for hours. He enjoyed his sandwich, chips and cold drink. Walter and Sylvester sat down and prepared sandwiches to eat. They also had chips and cold drinks.

After the three men ate and rested, they decided to go back and use ropes and anchor hooks to climb up the deep hole. It took four hours to climb up the crevices and ledges as they pulled themselves up the hole. Jerry slipped several times and almost fell. Walter used a long rope and stakes to retrieve Jerry. Sylvester followed Jerry and Walter until they all reached the top of the deep hole. They managed to climb out of this hole.

Jerry, Walter and Sylvester brought the gems and special stones in sacks with them. These gems and stones were valuable. The explorers were fortunate that the snakes crawling about deep in the Earth didn't bite any of them.

Jerry, Walter and Sylvester learned more about the interior of the Earth. They realized that caverns can and do exist deep within the Earth. Many precious gems and stones plus gold exists deep within the Earth.

THREE

THE MOON TODAY AND THE FUTURE

The Moon revolves around the Earth. The Moon is 250,000 miles from our Earth. The Earth only has one Moon. Only the part of the Moon reflecting sunlight toward Earth can be easily seen by Earthlings. The other side is turned away from the Sun and is very dark and cold.

The Moon revolves around the Earth every 28 days. On a clear night, the Moon appears brightly shining as the result of reflected sunlight toward Earth. There are several different phases of the Moon. They are full Moon, a gibbous Moon, a half Moon, a quarter Moon and a crescent Moon appearing each month.

The Moon has been photographed by NASA and astronauts. Scot Carpenter, Edgar Mitchell, Buzz Aladrin and Neil Armstrong landed on the Moon in 1969. Neil

Armstrong said, "One small step for man—one giant step for mankind," as he stepped onto the Moon.

The Moon today is still observed by astronauts, scientists and people in general. Craters are seen on the surface of the Moon. There is no life on the Moon. A Moon station has been established on the Moon.

Scientists realize that it is useless to form colonies on the Moon because there is no known oxygen or water. Plants could only grow in sealed domes. Water and oxygen would have to be supplied regularly to any plant domes. This would cost a lot because many trips to the Moon would be necessary.

Recent scientific news reveals that the Moon is becoming hollow inside and it may spin out of balance if the magnetism in the Moon becomes more imbalanced. Because the Moon is a dying planet this could happen at any time.

Is there anything world scientists and NASA can do to avoid the Moon colliding with the Earth someday? With today's space technology we don't know how to avoid what might happen on the Moon. It is too large for Earthlings to control. Let's hope the Moon will not spin out of orbit for a long time into the future.

FOUR

MIRACLES WORK

Most people think there are few or no miracles that take place in the world. However, we have learned that miracles are experiences that seem impossible to happen.

How do you explain how a crippled person walks again after prayers have been offered and healing hands have been placed on the crippled location in the body? How do we understand that a blind person from birth can suddenly see?

There have been a variety of such miracles that have taken place throughout history. Giving birth to more than four babies seems like a miracle. Some women have given birth to six babies. All these babies survived and are living.

We need to have faith and belief in miracles so that they can take place. Open-minded people tend to experience miracles.

We hear about someone who fell off of a very high building and survived it without serious injuries. This seems to be a miracle. Most people who fall off of a very high building usually are killed because of so many wounds.

Some people have been stranded on the ocean hundreds of miles away from civilization or the nearest shore. Yet, some people have managed to swim hundreds of miles until they reach land. It seems like a miracle that anyone can survive such an ordeal.

Mountain climbers experience many dangers while climbing up high mountains like Mt. Everest and The Alps. Some mountain climbers have encountered glaciers on mountaintops. Glaciers tend to melt and slide down steep slopes of the mountains. Many mountain climbers have been killed because of sliding glaciers.

Yet, the newspapers report that some mountain climbers have survived glacier sliding. They manage to recover from dangerous falls without a scratch. This could be a miracle.

Miracles occur here and there. When they occur people are amazed and surprised. Miracles are rare but they do happen. Miracles seem impossible. Yet, when a possible miracle takes place it makes people think and wonder about such experiences.

FIVE

GARDEN SOLARIUMS

Garden solariums are usually well organized. Planets are kept in enclosed domes with warm air. Garden solariums exist in many places in the world.

At Kew Gardens in London, England there are solariums known as hot houses containing a variety of plants and flowers. There are solariums for tropical plants.

It is best to keep desert and tropical plants in protective environments in England because the climate is too damp and cold. Some plants do not survive in extremely hot climates either. The sun is too hot and there isn't enough water in severely hot climates. Plants in general have to acclimate to such a climate to survive.

Garden solariums can be arranged in a beautiful manner. Visitors can stroll through solarium, hot houses. There are a variety of desert cacti and desert trees such as yuccas, palm trees and desert shrubs, which are protected in solariums in very cold climates. Tropical flowers such as orchids, birds of paradise and lilies, etc. grow well in solariums. They are able to remain healthy in a warm environment in the solariums.

Golden Gate Park in San Francisco, California has botanical solariums. Many tropical plants are grown in these warm solariums. Many visitors tour through these well-known botanical solariums to enjoy looking at the hundreds of colorful, tropical plants in their specific environments.

Central Park in New York City has botanical solariums because of the seasonal climatic changes. Tropical and desert plants live in a warm indoor, solarium climate. People can enjoy viewing these many varieties of plants and flowers.

SIX

ARCHITECTURAL WONDERS

The Empire State Building was one of the first high-rise buildings to be built in New York City in New York State. There are 102 stories in this building. It is lit up at night so many residents and visitors can enjoy the dazzling lights from this building.

The Space Needle Tower in Seattle, Washington is another architectural wonder. This spaceship shaped building is held up by a tower platform. At the top of this spaceship shaped building overlooking the surrounding area one can see spectacular views for miles. Elevators carry visitors up to the top into the round spaceship building and back down again. Once inside, one can observe breathtaking views through the many panoramic windows that surround the building 360-degrees. Scientific displays are arranged in a large room in the Space Needle. You can step outside onto a terrace and walk around the circular building.

The Top of the Mar in San Francisco, California is another wonder. There is a revolving room at the top of this tall building. You can look at a spectacular view of San Francisco through large windows. People go up to the top of the Mar for dinner and drinks. You can see San Francisco lit up with gleaming lights for miles.

Frank Lloyd Wright has constructed many award-winning, architectural structures for both commercial and residential buildings. He personally designed and created such unique, design styles that are very different and unusual so he was highly sought after by the rich and famous for their own personal structures. During his professional life span, Frank Lloyd Wright received many recognitions, citings and awards. There also have been several prime time documentaries recognizing his talent and skills.

Frank Lloyd Wright changed structural-design traditions by creating multiple, floor levels in one room and hugh bay windows, floor-to-ceiling window and wall panels. He was the first structural architect to make use of natural lighting by utilizing special, protective, roof-placed, glass windows to illuminate interior living area rooms. Also, he employed the theory of the sun's overhead path to provide morning sunlight for kitchens and breakfast rooms and bedrooms to late afternoon, natural lighting for living rooms and patio areas. Whether it was single-family homes or skyscrapers, each of his drawings, were different and unique from one another ranging from futuristic, modern, New England, colonial, ranch to oriental styles. Each has won for him worldwide recognition, awards and contracts from time to time.

Pyramids of Egypt are considered unusual, architectural wonders. These pyramids are the highest stone type structures in Egypt. The question that concerns engineering minds. How did Egyptians in that time period manage to build such large and precise structures without the use of modern day, engineering technology or building tools is remarkable?

In Dubai near the Persian Gulf, the King Abdullah of Dubai is building very unusual, high-rise hotels and residential buildings. He is now building mammoth size, permanent islands in the shape of palm trees to build residential neighborhoods with plush-looking home design for Dubai's elite class. King Abdullah makes no excuses for attempting to draw business from around the world to his island paradises knowing some day a land rich in oil revenues could soon play out. He is now building for future revenue earning possibilities for Dubai's future economic growth and sustainability.

The United Nations Building stands out in New York Harbor. Many windows exist, which shine in the daily sky. This modern, high-rise building has over 125 floors.

The tallest skyscraper in the world is being constructed at Burj Dubai set to open later this year in 2009. This skyscraper points very high in the sky and has many stories.

SEVEN

FASCINATING MINERALS AND GEMS

Fascinating minerals are gold, silver, zinc, iron, copper, quartz, nickel lead and aluminum. Gold and silver are especially valued. They are used to make jewelry. Silver is used to make silverware, trays, plates, cups and some other household items.

Gold rings are popular. Wedding rings are made of gold as well as silver. Gold necklace, bracelets and anklets are very dazzling and shiny. Copper pots and pipes are considered to be valuable. Quartz can be polished and made into rings, brocades and broaches.

Precious gems are diamonds, opals, crystals, jade rubies, sapphires, rhinestones, etc. Diamonds are considered to be very valuable. Diamonds are processed into rings, necklaces and bracelets. Diamonds are used to design wristwatches and other items.

Opals, jade, rubies, sapphires and rhinestones can be used to make rings. These precious gems are polished to shine brightly.

Minerals and gems are worth having as valuable and useful keepsakes or investments. Many minerals and gems are expensive usually. As buyers and investors we are fascinated with adornments for their bright, sparkling colors and dazzling appearance.

EIGHT

WOMEN AND MEN'S FASHIONS

Clothing fashions continue to change from generation to generation. Clothes designed and worn in the 1920s are very different then what we wear today. People in the 1930s continued to wear new fashions. Women and men's clothing fashions continued to change in the 1940s, 1950s, 1960s, 1970s, 1980s, 1990s, and 2000 and so on.

Women in the 21st Century wear a variety of clothing. Women can wear long dresses such as Afghans, shifts, mu-mus and other long dresses. Pantsuits are popular. Shorts and shorter pants are worn. Women wear sleeveless blouses and dresses. Cardigan sweaters are not worn as much anymore.

Women wear bikinis often at the beach. This swimsuit style began in the 1940s and was a one-piece suit covering the body. Today two piece-bikinis only cover ones private areas. It is still popular especially in the South Sea Islands and other warmer areas to permit topless swimwear styles for the sun worshipers of the world.

Jackets are worn over clothes. Women and men now wear very casual clothing such as sweatshirts, men's shirts and blue jeans. Of course, less casual clothing to formal wear is still worn when the occasion calls for it.

Men wear casual shirts or T-shirts with blue jeans or shorts almost everywhere. They wear tennis shoes. Sports jackets are popular with T-shirts or sports shirts and men's slacks. Formal suits are rarely worn today. Men wear formal suits to weddings, graduations and sometimes to funerals.

Men wear bright and cheerful colors as pink, purple, orange and other colors as maroon, lime green and red. Men are willing to wear different kinds of pants or blue jeans, too.

Men wear daring, skimpy, bathing shorts today providing their physic accommodates them. Wear these revealing swim shorts to appear sexy. They wear bright colored swimwear. Hats are popular to wear as well. Men wear baseball hats; straw hats and few men wear formal, dress hats. In Europe, top hats and sports hats are more commonly worn.

Clothing styles will continue to change from generation to generation. Color schemes, clothing designs and clothing sizes vary. Each person has the choice to select clothing they like best. People are flexible about clothes they want to wear.

NINE

PHENOMENAL CHANGES

Changes are expected in our lives. We get used of things being the way we like them to be. Then, suddenly something happens to come along to change our routines and daily experiences.

A phenomenal change usually is more dramatic then an ordinary change. Something phenomenal is unusual and striking. We respond to spectacular events and experiences.

Dolores Egan was a creative, adventurous person. She was an independent, imaginative and soul-searching individual. Dolores enjoyed new adventures. She was used to sudden changes. She remembered when her mother past away one day a few years ago.

Dolores was in her mother's bedroom when she witnessed her mother's death. She observed how her mother was conscious and was breathing. The next minute her mother stopped breathing. Her mother's eyes stopped moving and became lifeless. Her life's energy had left her mother's body.

Dolores sat in her mother's room for a while and looked at her. She finally decided to leave her mother's bedroom. So, Dolores had to adjust to the fact that her mother had past away at age 76.

Dolores went outside in the garden several days later for a stroll near some fragrant flowers and green leafy trees. She was trying to accept her mother's death. As she walked along she observed butterflies and bees flying around in the garden.

While Dolores was gazing at the garden she began to recall the many good times she had enjoyed doing things with her mother while she was alive. Suddenly, her mother appeared before Dolores in her astral form. Dolores was surprised, yet pleased to see her mother.

Dolores stared at the astral image of her mother. Her mother was dressed in a lavender dress. Her face appeared radiant and angelic like. Her mother smiled at Dolores. She appeared much younger and happier.

Dolores spoke to her mother and hoped she could hear her speak. Dolores said, "Mother, how are you? I didn't expect to see you ever again." Dolores mother replied, "I am happy. I know I have passed from the physical plane. I feel much better now. Be happy for me."

Dolores began to cry. She realized her mother was trying to cheer her up. Dolores finally spoke again to her mother. She said, "I hope you are happy. You look much younger and freer from concern. I miss you. We have shared so much together."

Dolores' mother suddenly disappeared. Dolores stood there and realized that her mother was in another dimension and that she was finally happier. Dolores tried to adjust to her mother's passing. She had just witnessed a phenomenal change in her life. She hoped to continue to be able to communicate with her mother from another dimension.

TEN

TEENAGE BEHAVIOR

Teen years are challenging years for parents usually because hormones in one's body are changing. Teenagers go through emotional stresses and struggles driving parents crazy at times. Some teenagers break out in pimples and blemishes because of hormone imbalances during the teen period of their lives.

Teenage girls generally mature faster than teenage boys. Girls start their period at age eleven or twelve. Once a girl has periods her body continues to mature. She can become pregnant if she engages in sexual intercourse.

Teenagers like to date each other when they are in high school and in college during their late teen years. It's a period of discovery for them. They are attracted to the opposite sex. Some teenagers experience sexual involvement at a much earlier age.

Some teenage girls become pregnant out of wedlock. Some teenage girls have not learned to use birth control methods. As a result many of them are victims of unwanted pregnancy.

Teenagers have a lot to learn about life. Learning to get along with one another is important. Some teenagers have difficulty relating to others. These teenagers have to learn to adjust to life. While they make many acquaintances, they may have few friends.

Some teenagers are more mature than other teenagers. They grow up sooner than other teenagers. Some teenagers accept responsibilities early in life, making more mature choices while others seem never to grow up being child-like into their adult years. Each mature choice helps a teenager grow up faster.

Some teenagers cope with challenges and problems better than other teenagers. Because they are able to cope with problems and challenges with better conduct, they are able to accomplish a lot more.

Teenagers outgrow childish ways and emotional imbalances once they become adults. However, many adults still experience certain immaturities. We go through different stages in order to reach adulthood.

ELEVEN

COLLEGE SEMINARS

Universities and colleges generally have specific seminars for different topics and issues. Seminars are presented so that well organized lectures are presented by qualified speakers. Seminars are valuable because participants are able to learn more about given subjects and issues.

Seminars are held for Education, Psychology, Social Science, Agriculture, Economics, Mathematics, Science and other topics. Specialized lectures are presented for each subject.

Many college students and professors become involved at college seminars. Students go to certain seminars based on their college majors and interests as an additional mode of learning. Often, students take notes while they listen to lectures. They are able to refer to their notes, which can be of benefit to them in their college courses in their field and major.

Usually new books and pamphlets are displayed on tables. These book and pamphlets are available for college students to purchase. These books and pamphlets are useful because of the knowledge and information they provide for those who purchase them.

College seminars are usually presented throughout the college school year so students can be enriched by extracurricular knowledge. Professors, who are well known around the world, participate in seminars during different times of the school year.

Visual aids, films, charts and bulletin boards are generally used at seminars. These visual materials add to the enrichment of the seminars. Films and pictures add a great deal to seminars. The participants are motivated by visual stimulation.

Up-to-date issues are presented at seminars so that college students can be informed about current situations and happenings in the world. It is worth attending seminars.

TWELVE

PRIVATE MOMENTS

Everyone has private moments in his or her life. When a person goes to bed in his or her private bedroom this is a time for privacy as a rule. Here is a time to be alone to think, contemplate about the next day, rest, dream and do private activities.

If a person lives in a large family there usually is little privacy because children share bedrooms and husbands and wives share a bedroom. Therefore, private moments occur when a person usually is resting in bed and everyone else is asleep.

Mary Jane Tompkins was an only child. Her parents were wealthy and they were prominent in the town where she lived in. Mary Jane had a lot of time by herself to use her imagination. Her parents were busy with civic and social events most of the time. She was a lonely child because she spent so much time by herself.

She played with her dolls and toys. She pretended to be a mother when she played with her dolls.

Mary Jane had dolls that could cry, wet the bed and looked like real babies. She held each baby doll in her arms gently. The baby dolls generally wet their diapers. If they cried she pretended to calm them down because she pretended they were real.

During private moments Mary Jane continued to use her imagination. She pretended that she was a princess in a castle. She decided to dress up in a fancy, long dress made of silk and satin with lace rimmings. She had a doll carriage for her baby dolls. She decided to dress some of her dolls. She placed them into the baby carriage.

It was a sunny day so Mary Jane decided to roll the baby carriage with her dolls outside into the garden. The outdoor garden was enormous with a variety of colorful flowers and flowering scrubs. Mary Jane strolled her baby carriage implanted pathway in this beautiful garden. She smelled the fragrance of roses daffodils, sunflowers, daisies poppies and lilacs there.

As Mary Jane walked around in the large garden she came to a serene pond. Running water was flowing in a miniature waterfall. Mary Jane stopped at the pond. She watched small goldfish and carps swimming about the dark blue pond. Plants grew around the pond. Mary Jane continued to observe many fish moving around the pond.

Finally, strolling around the grounds of her parents' three-story estate, she saw several colorful butterflies flittering onto branches and flowers. One was a bright gold with purple design. Another butterfly was bright orange with black geometric designs. Mary Jane was fascinated with the butterflies. She tried to capture some of them. They all flew away and escaped from Mary Jane

Mary Jane continued to walk down the pathway until she came to a grove of evergreen trees. She sat down under one of the shady trees. She placed the doll carriage nearby before she sat down. As she sat down leaning against the sturdy, leafy tree she gazed around the grove. Her parents had a 10-acre estate. She smelled the fragrant evergreen leaves and surrounding grasses and wild flowers in this peaceful grove.

As Mary Jane rested under the comfortable tree she dozed off into a slumber. She began to dream. She dreamt that she was in an enchanted forest. The enchanted forest sparkled with vibrant, bright light with rays of yellow, purple, pink and green. Mary Jane experienced and uplifting feeling. She saw fairies flying around in this enchanted forest. They were singing celestial songs. Their voices were high pitched, yet very melodic.

Mary Jane dreamt that a fairy king and queen appeared before all the rest of the other fairies. They were dressed in golden robes and wore golden crowns with sparkling diamond light emanating from their crowns. They stood before the fairies and the fairy king commanded that the fairies come to quiet attention. All the fairies sat down in a circle and looked at the fairy king and fairy queen.

The fairy king welcomed Mary Jane to come sit in the groups. She sat among the fairies. The fairy king and fairy queen accepted Mary Jane. The fairy king spoke, "Welcome. We accept newcomers to our fairyland. Where do you come from?" Mary Jane smiled and replied, "I am from around here. My parents and I live here. This forest—grove is within our 10-acre estate. So, here I am. Thank you for welcoming me."

The fairy king and fairy queen began to sing melodically. All the fairies began to sing. Mary Jane decided to sing and she listened to the fairies. Her voice was deeper and louder than the fairies. She felt happy because the fairies had accepted her and allowed her to join them.

Mary Jane suddenly awoke. She looked around and realized that she had been dreaming. She wished that she could see the fairies again. She stood up and strolled the baby carriage with her baby dolls back to her parents' home. She walked into the house.

Mr. and Mrs. Tompkins had come home. Mary Jane was glad to see them. She told them about her dream about the fairies. They smiled and knew she had recalled a dream.

Mary Jane went to her bedroom to put her dolls away. She placed the baby carriage in the corner of her bedroom. She decided to lay down on her bed and she thought about her experience with the fairies in the enchanted forest. She hoped to see and hear their melodic voices once again.

THIRTEEN

LIBRARIANS SUCCEED

Librarians have important responsibilities and duties. There are college librarians and public librarians. Librarians also work in specialized firms and departments.

A librarian is able to locate books by topics and authors. Reference librarians are able to look up reference books such as encyclopedias, dictionaries, telephone books, index books, catalogues and various books.

Librarians guide library patrons in locating library books. Books are stacked on shelves from A to Z. Some books are shelved by authors. Local authors and well-known authors are put in special locations in libraries.

College students do research in their chosen fields and subject matter. These students ask reference librarians to help them gather research books to use in their projects and research reports.

Librarians are successful because they are able to locate worthwhile information and knowledge to help their library patrons. Librarians update libraries with new and current books, magazines and reference books.

Libraries are cultural centers for presentations of poetry, stories and new books. Poets and other writers are asked to present their original writings. Librarian often present books and some librarians read stories to children in the children's section on a regular basis.

Librarians are successful at serving the public by enlightening patrons about different books, magazine and reference books.

FOURTEEN

LAWYERS APPEAL CASES

Lawyers accept different legal cases. A lawyer interviews a client to find out why the client needs legal support. The specific case is carefully reviewed and discussed in full detail. The lawyer then determines what to do to win a case.

The client is required to be honest and state any and all facts and specific details as well as proof regarding incidents related to the case presented. The lawyer develops a strategy in order to present the client's case in court. It is necessary to develop evidence and to seek witnesses who will testify about the truth in court.

Sometimes witnesses are subpoenaed so they must go to court to testify. The client may be called to the stand to answer questions. Both of the lawyers, for the opposing position and defense position, are allowed to ask questions as well as to make statements. Each lawyer makes final statements to the judge and jury. A jury of twelve jurors must decide whether a defendant is guilty or not guilty.

Many cases are lost. When a case is lost a client has the right to appeal the case. The lawyer tries to set up the case in a higher court or a different court. The case is reviewed once again to a different judge and jury. The lawyer presents the evidence again. Hopefully, stronger evidence exists so the client has a better chance to win.

Even during an appeal made for a given case the client may lose again. If the case is lost it cannot be reviewed and presented again. If the case is won then the case is dismissed. The client is free to leave court without having to go to jail or to go to court regarding this same case again.

FIFTEEN

PRESENTING A SPEECH

The delivery of a speech makes a difference to the audience. How a person presents a speech has an emotional effect and impact on each person in the audience.

The subject matter, tonal quality, cadence and the amount of volume all effects listeners' responses. If the speaker is not energetic and dramatic enough and speaks softly, the audience soon loses attention and interest in his or hers speech presentation.

Speakers need to select stimulating and interesting topics to hold the listeners interest. Great orators are effective, dramatic speakers. How he or she dresses and walks to the speaker's podium has a positive or negative effect on the audience.

Eye contact is important. Poor eye contact causes the audience to lose interest in the presentation. Use effective eye contact to keep you audience interested in your speech. Proper pronunciation is important and helps the audience to understand the speech. Clarification of speech affects the audience.

How a speaker begins speaking is vital because the beginning of a speech will determine how the audience responds. Start your speech with a dramatic beginning, middle and then end your speech with a convincing, dramatic close. In other words, tell them what you're going to tell them.

Great speakers arouse their audiences. They may cause a lot of responses and emotional impacts. What they have to say is important. The contents of a great speech should be filled with major ideas, examples and facts for the audience to mentally digest and think about. So, carefully prepare your speech. Be ready to deliver the speech effectively. Be willing to present a speech that awakens your audience. Present you speech with self-confidence.

SIXTEEN

SKIN CARE AND MAKEUP

We should take care of our skin. Our skin is the single largest body we have that protects our bodies from airborne bacteria, viruses and irritants. Our skin absorbs vitamin D sunlight while sweating out harmful body toxins and poisons. Our skin serves as a backup for our lungs and kidneys in that capacity.

We should always take the usual safety precautions to protect our skin from environmental and physical work and play damage. Women in general do a much better job at this with frequent washing of hands and later applying protective vitamin or medicated creams or gel coats. This means using sunscreen, too.

Some women and men are able to restore their skin by using skin application and treatments with heat and topical rejuvenators. These may be Aloe Vera to a wide range of other botanical plants that posses curative components. These kinds of plants contain safety from hazards in the wild. But when tamed and properly processed will have most beneficial and curative qualities that can assist in healing a broad range of health issues.

Many skin care products can be acquired from your local retailers to mass merchandisers like Wal-Mart, K-Mart, Rite Aide, CVS pharmacies to name a few. Other such stores are Ross For Less, Macy's, to Maxwell's and Target Stores. All carry and display a good selection of skin care products.

Select skin care products carefully. Some skin products may not have the best ingredients to use on your skin. Read the ingredients on the bottles of any first time new skin care products before buying them. Once you have used any such products, observe how the skin care product performs and the affects it has on your body. If you break out with blemishes and your skin appears discolored you should stop using a skin care product, which may be causing a problem.

Makeup should be carefully selected. Makeup, which dries or cakes up on your skin, should not be used. Natural ingredients to cover up your skin are best to use. You need to protect your face when you use makeup of any kind.

Cover Girl and Revlon makeup have been recommended to use on your face for years. Carefully apply makeup as recommended by the manufacturer. Apply healing skincare creams. Watch for possible negative affects. Allow your skin to be restored before applying makeup again on your facial skin that can be maintained with youthfulness.

SEVENTEEN

MOVIE STARS DISILLUSION US

Movie stars are capable of pretending to be someone else. They act out a given role in a film. Each actor and actress must behave according to the given script.

Actors and actresses learn dialogue in scripts. They behave a certain way on stage or in a movie set. They follow the director's instructions. Tone of voice, facial expressions and stage movements are important.

A movie star may act very different in real life than he or she acts in a movie or stage play. When we go to the movies we experience illusions about life. We pretend the movies we see are real while we use our imagination. We can be disillusioned while we watch different movies. We should carefully select the movies we watch and focus on.

Henry Fonda, who became a superstar, played many different roles such as, war heroes, patriotic leaders, and many romantic roles, too. He appeared self-confident while acting movie parts. However, in his personal life he was shy, withdrawn and unsociable.

Michael Jackson the self-proclaimed "King Of Rock," after his super-hit movie, <u>Thriller</u>, became worldwide and famous for his many dance routines and vocal interpretations. He aroused many people within his audiences because of his unique costumes and grand, performance productions. However, in his personal life he was shy and withdrawn, accused of being gay, but he was married twice and had children. He had many facial, plastic surgeries in attempt to change his appearance to become more attractive.

Marilyn Monroe became a sex symbol in the 1950s. She was trained by acting coaches to speak and walk a sexy manner. She dressed sexy and wore sexy hairdos. In her personal life she was intellectual and career minded. She never had any children. Her life ended in a tragic death. So, we can conclude that actors and actresses may portray certain movie characters in stageplays or in theater roles. Yet, in their personal life they acted totally opposite as serious individuals.

EIGHTEEN

USING DIFFERENT MAPS

Maps are very useful because we can look up continents, islands, oceans, seas and zones as well as locate the equator, which divides the world in two the upper and lower halves. There are different kinds of maps referred to when geographers, archeologists, scholars and people in general study maps.

Paper, flat maps can be folded and carried around so those using them may use them readily wherever they travel to a specific location. Globes are dimensional, round shapes with oceans, seas, continents, zones as well as the equator and North and South Poles.

Flat maps are spread out more because they are flat. The North and South Poles are designated. Continents are shown, vividly labeled with name of cities, rivers and mountains. Maps are shown in atlases and reference, map books. Up-to-date atlases show the most recent towns, cities and other locations.

Maps are made to show detailed descriptions of city streets, town streets and freeways. You can purchase city maps and state maps at gasoline stations. Atlases are available at bookstores. Atlases are published annually with new additions so map users may look up recent details on newer maps.

Maps are very useful when people travel long distances. A map user can follow information about interstate freeways so they can go on freeways indicated on state maps. Routes, junctions and regular freeways are described. Some specific maps describe railroad connections.

Keep travel maps in your car or van to use when you travel long distances. City maps are very useful to use as well. You can trace specific streets so you can go to different places in a city with the correct directions by reading a city map for street directions.

NINETEEN

RAISING A GIFTED CHILD

Some children are brighter than others. The brighter a child is, the more he or she needs to develop his or her abilities and talents.

Parents should provide stimulating activities and cultural enrichment for their children. Surround your bright child with worthwhile reading materials, creative experiences and of course—computers. Children, who are given the opportunity to develop their abilities, are more fulfilled at an earlier age.

When a child develops his or her talents, these talents may be of benefit in their adult life. For instance, when a child learns to play the piano early he or she can learn to play more advanced pieces sooner. Playing the piano is a creative and worthwhile experience. An accomplished pianist can play many piano pieces well. He or she can perform publically at community events, at church and school as well as make a career as a pianist.

Some children have good singing voices. A child can take voice lessons at age 10 and up to learn to develop his or her voice. As a vocal soloist a person can perform in operas, light musicals, concerts and at other public events. A vocal career can be worthwhile to pursue.

Becoming an artist is another creative experience. Children can be taught to draw, paint and to make sculptures with clay. With art lessons and instructions a child can learn to become a very good artist. Professional artists are able to earn a lot of money by selling their paintings. Sculptors also can make money for their sculptures.

Children can be taught to write poetry, short stories, plays and novels. Writing techniques and skills can be developed. A child can become a good writer. Gifted children are able to write more advanced writings. They can become professional writers. Some gifted writers become famous for their writings.

Gifted children need more stimulating projects and more challenging experiences in order to fulfill themselves. Their special gifts can be expressed through creativity and worthwhile experiences.

TWENTY

SCHOOL DAY EXPERIENCES

Schooldays are opportunities for us to learn as much as possible about many things. We have the chance to learn all we can about many subjects and to discuss many issues about a variety of topics. We can express our ideas in different classrooms at different grade levels.

We are concerned about passing each subject with good grades. Most students want to earn (A)s and (B)s. We want to be accepted and to succeed in school. Our teachers establish goals for us to achieve in school.

Each elementary grade offers specific experiences so we can learn to read, write and do arithmetic, to work in groups and to do artwork as well as play physical education games. As we progress through school we become more advanced in academic skills and social awareness. We learn many games and how to exercise well. We need to exercise in order to maintain good health.

In school we have the opportunity to make friends. We can continue to develop new friendships. A personal relationship with others adds to our awareness of human behavior and attitudes. We learn from others how to behave. We need to communicate so we can express our inner most feelings.

School provides a place for us to grow and develop year by year. We mature in different stages according to our experiences. We learn from our mistakes as well as accomplishments.

Life itself is a schoolroom in progress. We learn from daily experiences how to communicate and to relate to others. We can learn different skills and we can specialize in given fields. We have an opportunity to learn as much as possible.

TWENTY-ONE

WHAT IS BEAUTIFUL?

What is beautiful? Gaze at sunlight rays through tree branches and silhouetting trees. Observe a clear blue sky. Enjoy designs of rose petals in brightly colored roses. Look at flowering trees and scrubs. You will be able to see the natural beauty of nature.

Go for a stroll through an evergreen forest or grove. Notice blue-green leaves swaying in the breeze. See many grasses, lichen and sword ferns growing in the ground creating a natural carpet, which covers the forest floor.

Beauty is in the mind of the beholder. We all see beautiful things. We appreciate beautiful designs and shapes. We enjoy looking at beautiful ocean scenes, sunsets, nature scenes of gardens and landscapes.

The shapes of flowers and vivid colors in flowers are magnificent to observe. Yellow-green leaves swaying in the breeze stimulate our sense of colors and nature designs Daffodils bob in the wind. Purple lilacs arouse our eyes because of their sheer beauty.

Certain birds emanate bright colors. Parrots and parakeets are vivid green, yellow and orange. Peacocks display their magnificent plumes majestically. Some birds chirp melodically with beautiful tones. Deer move swiftly through acres of green, swaying, grass fields.

Vivid sunsets arouse us with their bright orange, red, yellow, and purple hues. We feel rapture when we hear beautiful voices creating very melodic sounds. We have much to be thankful for when we observe the natural beauty of this Earth.

TWENTY-TWO

BEAUTIFUL AUSTRALIA

Australia, the largest island continent, is known as the land down under. Australia has many wonders to behold. You can meet Aborigines who are descendants of ancient Aborigines who have lived in Australia for over 30,000 years. Aborigines paint their faces and worship their ancient gods. Ancient Aborigines lived in the outback in deserts and caves. They painted ancient drawings of people and animals in many caves.

Kakadu National Park is where many Aborigines live Australia's Northern Territory. The Aborigines are the ancient people of Kakadu. The Aborigines continue to learn tribal language.

Australia means "southern." Australia has 16,000 miles or 25,760 km of coastline. Australia is surrounded by the Indian Ocean. Major cities are Sydney, Perth, Adelaide, Melbourne, Brisbane Murray and Darwin in

Australia. There are large, sandy deserts such as Tanami Desert, Great Sandy Desert, Gibson Desert, Nullarbor Plain and Simpson Desert.

Most of the highlights are along the coast of Australia. Lake Mackay, Lake Eyre and Lake Torrens are beautiful where residents and tourists go boating and fishing. The Great Dividing Range is in the Northeastern region near the Great Barrier Reef near the Coral Sea.

Most of the highlights are along the coasts of Australia. Lake Mackay, Lake Eyre and Lake Torrens are beautiful where residents and tourists go boating and fishing. The Great Dividing Range is in the Northeastern region near the Great Barrier Reef near the Coral Sea.

Australia is divided into six states and two mainland territories. Almost all their borders are perfectly straight, down along lines of latitude and longitude. Western Australia covers the western one third of the continent. Down the center are the Northern Territory and South Australia. The eastern third is Queensland, New South Wales, Victoria and Tasmania. The tiny Australian Capital Territory is totally surrounded by New South Wales.

The eastern edge of Australia is the eastern highlands region, the nation's best farmland. The region runs all the way from northern Queensland's Cape York Peninsula to southern Tasmania. Lush rain forests once existed in the eastern highlands before cities and farms were developed in their place. There are rain forests still in unsettled parts of the region.

Along the Pacific Coast there are magnificent beaches and jagged cliffs. Most of the population exists in Brisbane, Sydney, Melbourne and Canberra in Australia.

The eastern highlands are also called the Great Dividing Range. It is a stretch of hills and plateaus covered with grasslands and forests. Australia's highest mountains are the Australian Alps. They rise at the south end of the Great Dividing Range. Australians and tourists love to ski in the Snowy Mountains, the highest range in the Australian Alps. Australia's tallest peak is Mount Kosciusko, which rises in the Snowies.

The island of Tasmania, part of the Great Dividing Range, is a land bridge once connecting the mainland. Now the Bass Strait flows between Australia and Tasmania. Southwestern Tasmania is a wilderness of rugged mountains, river rapids and thundering waterfalls.

Vast expanses of desert take up the central part of the western plateau. There is the Great Victoria Desert in the south, the Gibson Desert in the center and the Great Sandy Desert to the North. Farther north still is the Tanami Desert. At the Northern Territory's Top End are Arnhem Land and the city of Darwin.

Along the southern coast is the Nullarbor Plain. Nullarbor means "no trees" in Latin. East of the plain, the city of Adelaide spreads out along a bay. The Western plateau is dotted with astounding, rock formations. Right in the middle of Australia is the massive red rock called Uluru or Ayers Rock.

Uluru is a very large rock formation in the desolate center of Australia. An explorer named it Ayers Rock in 1873, after Henry Ayers, who was chief secretary of South Australia. Iron oxide in the sandstone gives the rock its blazing red-orange color. It rises 1,142 feet above the surrounding desert and a trip around its base is a 6-mile hike.

Uluru means "shadowy place," which is sacred to the Aborigines, who ask visitors not to climb the rock. In 1985 Ayers' Rock was returned to the Pitjantjatjare Aborigines, who were its original owners. The Aborigines live in the community of Mutiljulu at the base of the rock. They manage the rock with Australia's National Parks and Wildlife Service.

The Great Barrier Reef is a string of rock islands, which curves around Queensland's northeast coast for some 1,250 miles. The surrounding waters are called the Coral Sea. For millions of year's tiny sea creations called coral polyps, have lived off of Australia's northeast coast. When a polyps dies its skeleton remains on the ocean floor. Gradually, minerals in the seawater fill in the spaces where soft tissue had been. Over time the skeletons become as hard as rock. With each new generation, living polyps attach themselves to the old, bony layers of previous skeletons.

Layer after layer, the reef builds up until the highest mounds rise above the ocean surface. The Great Barrier Reef is the world's largest coral reef. Scientists from around the world come to study its animal and plant life. The Australian government and international conservation agencies are working to preserve this natural treasure.

Sydney, the capitol of New South Wales, is Australia's oldest and largest city. Two of its most famous landmarks, the Sydney Opera House and Sydney Harbour Bridge, lie along Sydney Harbour. The bridge leads to the rocks, where Australia's first settlers began their new life in 1788. This city center, Australia's economic hub, is built around Hyde Park. The Sydney tower exists here.

Melbourne, the capitol of Victoria, grew up around the Yarra River. It has modern buildings as well as old structures from the mining boom of the 1850's. Its metropolitan area is huge and much of it has lovely gardens and parks. Melbourne is home to many European and Asian people.

Brisbane, the capitol of Queensland, is near the Brisbane River. Brisbane's cultural center is a cluster of ultramodern buildings, which stand along side beautiful structures from earlier times such as the Old Government House and the Post Office.

Perth, the capital of Western Australia, sits at the mouth of the Swan River on the Indian Ocean. Perth is the business and shipping center for the state's mining industries. Buildings tower over the city center. Elegant old buildings line St. George's Terrace. Perth's attractions include the Hay and Murray Street shopping malls and Kings Park, with its elevated walkways through the treetops.

Adelaide, the capitol of South Australia, has been called the "city of churches." Today, modern high-rise buildings overshadow the early settler's churches and stone houses. The River Tarrens flows through Adelaide and beautiful parks and gardens surround the city.

Hobart, the city of Tasmania, is Australia's southern most city. It is near Mount Wellington where the Derwent River meets the Tasmania Sea. Hobert was an important whaling port in its early days. Old warehouses are now shops and restaurants along the cobblestone streets of Salamanca Place. The Tasmanian Museum and Art Gallery and the Maritime Museum cover the area's culture and history.

Australia has many wonders such as contrasting landscapes, cultural events and attractions. It is worth touring through Australia to enjoy its many attractions.

TWENTY-THREE

CLEANING HOUSE

Cleaning house can be an ordeal. However, it is necessary to clean house to maintain sanitation as well as to be neat. A clean house usually smells fresh. When furniture, sinks, toilets, tubs, showers and shelves are kept spotless our house looks good.

Usually housekeeping needs to be done every week. We need to vacuum carpets, remove soiled spots on carpets, mop kitchen and bathroom floors and clean our stoves, toaster and refrigerator. Our kitchen and bathrooms should be scrubbed and sanitized regularly.

It is important to know how to use a vacuum cleaner, to dust properly and to scrub sinks and toilets so that they shine and are kept white and nice. Clean kitchens and bathrooms help keep us healthier.

Housekeepers know how to select dish soap, sink detergents and dust polish. Tables and shelves can be kept clean and shiny when dust polish is used. Be sure to select dust polish, dish and toilet detergents with natural and nonpolluting ingredients at health food stores.

Parents usually teach their children how to clean house as they grow up. Girls usually become more proficient at cleaning house. They learn to wash dishes and dry them plus make beds. They learn to sweep floors and put toys and clothes away. Girls are generally neater than boys because they help around the house more

It is worthwhile to keep our homes clean and safe. After all, we live in our home on a regular basis. We are more comfortable and healthier when our homes are clean.

TWENTY-FOUR

PANORAMIC VISIONS

Panoramic visions are spectacular because a person can view magnificent scenery from a distance. Special views of the sunrays reflecting on mountainsides, slopes and peaks are magnificent to view.

Viewing vivid sunsets from a distance are spectacular moments. Bright colors producing colorful hues of light are creative designs to look at. Sunsets reflect in the ocean so we can see many vivid colors of orange, yellow, red, purple, etc.

When we can enjoy visions of flocks of golden geese reflected in the sunlight we look in awe. Pink flamingos flock together by the thousands. Their bright pink colors can be seen from a distance. Peacocks spread their plumes so we can enjoy looking at unusual color combinations.

From mountaintops and mountain peaks mountain climbers can see marvelous views of verdant valleys below. Take a helicopter ride to look at views of different landscapes up high in the sky. You will see panoramic views of valleys, beaches, oceans, forests and mountains. You can see rivers, creeks and streams following in a given direction. You can view many scenes of nature as well as towns, villages and even cities.

You can see different cloud formations in the sky. Some clouds look puffy while other clouds spread out and even look streaky. Clouds may change colors when the sunset reflects in them. There are pink and whitish-gray clouds with many creative patterns and designs. Clouds move across the sky. Some clouds are misty and drift over mountains hovering on mountaintops. Clouds over the ocean reflect different, interesting colors.

You can learn a lot by experiencing panoramic visions of fabulous scenery.

TWENTY-FIVE

MEXICO'S ENCHANTMENT

Mexico's is south of the United States of America. Mexico is surrounded by the Pacific Ocean and Gulf of Mexico. Three cultures and three identities exist in Mexico. In the heart of Mexico City there is a public square called the Plaza of Three Cultures. In one corner of the plaza are ruins of a pyramid built many hundreds of years ago by the Aztecs. The Spaniards built a gray stone church in the 1600s.

Today there are towering, modern buildings which exist in Mexico City. Almost all Mexicans have both indigenous and European ancestors. The church of Santiago was built in 1609. It is located in the Plaza of Three Cultures on top of the Aztec pyramid.

Modern Mexico City begins several blocks away from the old plaza. Traffic jams are now a problem in Mexico City. However, colorful flowerbeds grow in most Mexican households. Mexico is a land with contrasts high mountains, vast deserts and marvelous ocean beaches.

Mexico is a place where lively music and laughter exists. Music and festivals are a central part of life in Mexico. Dancers perform in the streets. The beach at Acapulco is lined with hotels. Millions of people come to Acapulco annually because it is a popular location.

Peaks of the Sierra Madre Occidental rise to between 5,000 feet to 10,000 feet. Mexico is a long, narrow country, which is narrow toward the southern half. Mexico has a landmass of 756,066 square miles which is the major portion of Central America which is between North and South America. Mexico is the fifth largest country in the Americas, after Canada, the United States, Brazil and Argentina.

Two enormous mountain ranges exist called the Sierra Madre Oriental and the Sierra Madre Occidental, which are the length of Mexico. A Plateau of Mexico lies between the two ranges. The Plateau of Mexico has steep hills, towering mountains and cone shaped volcanoes. The Plateaus of Mexico contains Mexico's best farming land and largest cities. Mountains meet the sea near Calvario Beach on the Pacific Ocean.

The longest river is Lemma River, which is 350 miles long. The Pacific Coast has more than 2,000 miles of seashores, which are along the West Coast of Mexico. In the south, the Yucatan Peninsula juts out to the east. Southern Mexico has rain forests and grassy plains, which spread across the land.

Mexico's warm climate causes people to live outdoors and to sell their fruits and vegetable out in the open. People on the Plateau of Mexico wear light clothing most of the time. Mexicans enjoy warm days at the beach. The ocean has beautiful, turquoise-blue water.

Guadalajara delights visitors with its fountains, public squares and tree-shaded parks. This city's restaurants are said to be the best in Mexico. A delicious stew called pozole is a favorite Guadalajaran dish.

Pueblo, Mexico's fourth-largest city has a strong Spanish influence. At least a thousand buildings from the Spanish colonial era exist in Central Pueblo. Many of those buildings are decorated with hand-painted tiles, which Pueblo is known for. This city is famous for a spicy sauce called poblano, which tastes a little like chocolate. More poblano is served over chicken than any other foods.

Some world-famous beach resorts are Acapulco and Cancun on the Gulf of Mexico. Acapulco became know in the 1940s. The most popular tourist spot in recent years is Cancun.

Mexicans know that much of their country rests on unstable ground. Mexico is even more earthquake prone than California. Mexico City is very earthquake prone.

Highways in Mexico now connect just about every corner of Mexico. The road system brings in farmers, businessmen and tourists to Mexico. A highway cuts across the Plateau of Mexico. More than 200,000 miles of roads crisscross Mexico.

The Copper Canyon is covered with forests of Ponderosa pine and oak. Deer, bear and mountain lions roam along the streams and in the pine forests. This canyon is home to about sixty thousand Tarahumara, an indigenous people who live mainly by farming and hunting. The Copper Canyon is a spectacular reminder of Mexico's wilderness in earlier times.

The plants and animals of Mexico's mountains are quite different than life on the seacoasts. The mountain environment has nurtured a fantastic variety of plant and animal life. Mexico's large wild animals such as deer, bears, bobcats and coyotes are ever present. Vultures circle around in the sky searching for dead animals to eat. Snakes, rodents and scurrying lizards are visible in the mountains.

The plateau of Mexico has few trees, but it is home to a huge variety of cactus plants. Nearly a thousand different kinds of cacti grow in the mountain regions. The saguaro or giant cactus grows very tall. It almost looks like a tree trunk without branches. Some saguaros reach a height of 50 feet. Prickly pear cactus is a help to farmers. They use barbed wire, sharp-quilted cactus, planted in rows to create fenced-off like pens to corral their cattle into sections.

Mexicans eat some cactus plants. A flat leaved cactus called nopal is stripped of its quills cut into tiny pieces and fried in oil. Fried nopal with scrambled eggs is often served for breakfast. A refreshing cactus fruit called tuna tastes like watermelon. The reddish tuna is covered with a fine coat of needle like quills, which can be peeled away only by experienced hands.

The lowlands in Mexico are in the south and west, which are swampy. Fruits such as mangos and papayas grow in the wetlands. Other fruits are bananas, oranges and grapefruits. After heavy rains, the southern wetlands are filled with flowers such as orchids, dahlias and bougainvilleas. Groves of coconut palm are standing along the beaches.

You will see herons, ducks and geese dwell about the lagoons at the wetlands. Flocks of pink flamingos feed in the swamps of the Yucatan Peninsula. The speckled ocelot, which looks like a large cat, still dwells in southern forests. Spider monkeys swing in trees in the forest. Iguanas exist which are large, green lizards with comb-like rows of scales running down its back. Alligators and poisonous snakes are also found in Mexico's tropics.

Spaniards brought donkeys to Mexico. The sturdy burro is a relative of the horse. The burro was used on Mexican farms and villages. There were shortages of burros in 2004. So, an official from the state of Jalisco imported fifty donkeys from Kentucky.

Tourism creates service jobs in hotels and restaurants. Mexico has a pleasant climate, friendly people, sparkling beaches and interesting ruins. For these reasons millions of visitors come to the sunny country year round. Mexico now ranks tenth in the world regarding tourism income. You can enjoy carnivals and festivals year round in Mexico. Mexico's enchantment will intrigue you as you travel to many exciting places around Mexico.

TWENTY-SIX

MODERN HOMES

Many modern houses have been built especially in cities around American. Modern houses have better features such as open wall kitchens, dining area and living room.

Newer bathroom facilities exist in many modern homes. Electric toilets automatic flush once you use them. More comfortable showers, with easy walk-ins and spas, better lighting, ceiling heaters, grab bars and built-in storage cabinetry are added to modern bathrooms.

Built-in television panels are installed in bedrooms, lounge rooms and even in living rooms. Large televisions are installed in modern homes. VCRs and DVDs are included and are used to play videos and disks.

Most modern homes have computers, dishwashers, microwave ovens and other modern, cooking facilities. Computers are now being used to perform a host of daily household tasks like controlling heating and cooling requirements, lighting, and security needs when the family is anticipating their next arrival to constantly anticipate these needs while the family is at home until they leave once again the following day. Computers will look up current daily news and any other specific information you may wish to have at your disposal at any given time of day or night you specify. At your convenience you can dictate any oral or written communications and have forwarded it to various, designated recipients at a time more convenient for them. The Internet provides for a communication highway that is efficient for both recipient and sender.

Modern, waterbeds to air filled, regulated mattresses are now available and merchandised. Mood lighting, piped in music to wall-mounted high-definition television monitors and space-saving storage cabinetry for personals and clothing items. Today computer technology is performing many kinds of useful mundane tasks not imagined a decade ago.

Central air and heating is usually a customary piece of equipment installed in today's modern homes. Solar energy is becoming more popular as an option for today's modern home. For instance, a large roof mounted solar system can be installed providing quality heat and cooling needs at modest costs. These improvements have a relative short-term investment cost payback for the modern homeowner. Of course, all this leads to families being able to save energy and avoid using natural gas and electricity. Money also can be saved by using modern solar energy technology.

Modern homes quite often have window roof panels for sky light views. People can look up at the sky view and see stars at night. During daylight hour's rays of the sun may beam into the homes providing needed light and heat various designated parts of the house.

Modern furniture is usually arranged in modern homes. Furniture is colorful, comfortable and very stylish and attractive. Colorful window coverings, floor coverings to paint décor are carefully and planned out. Clever real estate agents, attempt to entice perspective buyers into envisioning ownership, by using this same technique called staging. It's durable and very effective.

The exteriors of modern homes have changed as well. Exotic shapes of roofs and building pop-out designs are to be displayed. Use of materials, textures, colors, window shape and design, entrance and garage doors all add to a modern look in a home. The size and shape of a home is much more modern. More and more people are buying and living in more modern homes today.

TWENTY-SEVEN

CITY LIFE

City life is somewhat different than country life. There are many more public buildings, apartments and homes, etc. Many streets exist in cities. Some cities have high-rise structures. City streets are generally very busy.

There are many shops, stores and public businesses especially downtown in every city. Many people live in cities. People are strangers to each other. People live in suburbs and neighborhoods. Quite often neighbors don't even know one another.

Different sections exist in big cities. Suburbs surround the central area of each city. Public buses, transit systems, trolleycars and subways are used in cities. People can choose a bus or go on the Bart System instead of driving.

Crime may take place more often in cities because there are many more people. Gangs may develop in big cities. Los Angeles, California has many gangs problems regarding to various crimes occur. Gangs ten to cause violence and destruction of public property, etc. It is difficult to control crimes in big cities.

City life may offer many stimulating and cultural events and activities to attend. There are museums, art galleries, theatres, a variety of shops and stores to purchase a wide array of interesting items. A selection of restaurants is available so the residents and tourists can enjoy eating out. A variety of cuisines are served.

Public libraries, colleges and universities exist in big cities. These educational, public facilities are very valuable and useful. Students and the public in general can acquire knowledge and information at these institutions.

City life can be exciting because of many cultural and social events and activities and many other things there are to do. You can meet many interesting people in big cities at social functions at church and school. A person has an opportunity to experience many more worthwhile endeavors in cities.

Job opportunities are more available in cities. There are a variety of jobs and employment opportunities. A person can make better choices in selecting different occupations and careers. So, enjoy city life. You can go to parks, gardens and even zoos in big cities. You can enjoy a variety of cuisines at different city restaurants. Each city has its unique places and history. We can learn a lot when we live in a city. We have to get used of the noise and crowded conditions.

Generally, different ethnic groups live in big cities. Many ethnic and racial groups live in specific locations within cities such as New York City, San Francisco, Los Angeles and Chicago here in America. Ethnic groups have their own languages, cuisines and cultural beliefs and attitudes. Chinatown, Italian, Jewish, Black sections and other ethnic groups may exist in big cities. They must learn to accept and get along with each other.

TWENTY-EIGHT

MAINTAINING YOUR CAR

Repairing a car properly is important. The proper tools and equipment are necessary in order to repair any car. Mechanics need to know how to use mechanical tools. Whether basic hand-held tools to make a simple adjustment or advance, computer programs that display visual aid depicting all of the various parts of the whole including each nut, and bolt. For a complete maintenance of any car, all of the following tools and equipment are needed to keep an automobile repaired and operating in good order.

Most hand tools use U.S. or metric wrenches, sockets and combination open-end or box-ended wrenches from the smallest to largest. Other hand tools include a huge assortment of all kinds that usually filled multiple drawer tool cabinets on wheels to another assortment of larger ones hanging on a tool wall depending on what degree a mechanic practices repairs and rebuilds automobiles. A mechanic may easily have huge assortment of floor-mounted tools to large portable tool repair stations. Most auto manufacturers require necessary specialty tools that are pricey to acquire and maintain.

Because modern day mechanic shops requires such array of tools and knowledge to operate a full repair garage for all vehicles, mechanic professions demand advanced skills and knowledge to use all types of tools and computer programs housing a advanced library of repair information. Mechanics are now required to attend seminars, classes and specialty training courses. And for ongoing additional repair information that requires mechanics to pass state sponsored tests and licensing certifications.

A modern, mechanic, repair operations are beginning to look more like a doctors' office with attractively appointed waiting rooms, comfortable seating, carpeted floors, magazine racks, free coffee and water, snack machines, television, even background music in the work areas. With such repair operation and modern equipment, properly appointed trained and certified technicians come equally modern repair fees to support such a classy operation typically found at new car dealerships.

Large independent, auto repair businessmen are realizing the need for aspiring to this kind of contemporary, repair shops to attract a higher quality customer base who expects and is willing to pay for creature comforts while having their vehicles repaired.

Some of us can only afford a basic, shop businessman that can perform good reliable work at a fair price. A few businessmen are quietly offering auto repair financing for selected trustworthy customers because of higher costs.

Every car should be serviced and repaired regularly to help prevent mounting repairs costs. The rules of safety for mechanics range from DON'T smoke around gasoline, to use the proper tools for the job. The answer to avoiding injuries is to develop safe work areas, safe work habits and to take every possible precaution.

Do's that mechanics should follow include following rules. Do keep fire extinguishers and first aid kits within easy reach in a conspicuous location with proper warning signs. Mechanics should have safety glasses for vision protection while drilling, welding, cutting, grinding or prying, whenever you work around batteries. Batteries contain sulfuric acid. In case of contact with eyes or skin, flush the area with plenty of fresh water or a mixture of water and baking soda and seek medical attention immediately. Do use adequate ventilation when working with any chemicals. Do use protective goggles made from harden safety glass over their prescription glasses to protect the mechanics eyes.

A mechanics work could otherwise be interrupted if his or her sight is temporary or permanently damaged or lost. Mechanics must be safety and health conscious to stay employable, to earn money and support their families and to pay their bills and meet their other financial obligations.

When working with batteries, disconnect the negative cable post first. When working on anything electrical or near the electrical systems disconnect the negative cable post first. Do follow manufactures' directions whenever working with potentially hazardous materials. Do properly maintain your tools. They are your livelihood. Do use the proper size and type of tool for the job being done. Do pull on a wrench handle rather than push on it when possible and adjust your stance to prevent falling.

Do be sure that adjustable wrenches are tightly adjusted on the nut or bolt and pull so that the face is on the side of the fixed jaw. Select a wrench or socket that fits the nut or bolt. The wrench or socket set should sit straight, not cocked. Do strike squarely with a hammer to avoid glancing blows.

The energy that runs an internal combustion engine is heat created by the combustion of an air/fuel mixture. The combustion process takes place within a sealed cylinder containing a piston, which is able to move up and down in the cylinder. The piston is connected to a crankshaft by a connecting rod. The lower end of the rod is connected to the crankshaft at a point, which is offset from the centerline of the crankshaft, allowing it to turn a large circle. This is why a piston moves up and down and why pressure on the top of the piston eventually becomes torque, or turning force, for the crankshaft.

The car engine produces power from the combustion chamber that will have a tremendous affect on operating efficiency. An important aspect of engine overhaul work involves repair or replacement of parts so that the combustion chamber rings will be as tightly sealed as possible against the cylinder walls.

There are 2-stroke engines, and 4-stroke engines. In 4-stroke engines four strokes of events that occur in order for an engine to operate take place in one revolution of the crankshaft or it may take two revolutions of the crankshaft. The four events that must occur in order for an internal combustion engine to operate are intake, compression, power and finally exhaust. When all of these steps take place in succession, this is considered to be a four-stroke engine.

In a four-stroke engine, at top dead center, the first cycle, the intake valve opens allowing raw fuel/air mixture to be drafted into the piston chamber cavity as it travels in a downward motion creating a vacuum within the cylinder cavity. At button dead center, the second cycle, the intake valve closes. Then the piston rises toward the top again creating a tremendous amount of head pressure. This is called the compression stroke as the pressure continues to build until just before top dead center when an electric charge is sent to the spark plug and ignites the compressed fuel/air mixture followed by a tremendous explosion forcing the piston downward toward the bottom again. The third cycle is called the power stroke. At bottom dead center, the exhaust valve opens, the piston returns upward again. The fourth cycle takes place, forcing the burnt fuel/air mixture to be expelled through the open exhaust valve out the exhaust manifold and exhaust pipe as waste matter or carbon monoxide. Once the piston reaches top dead center again, the first, second, third, and fourth strokes or cycles repeat the process many times a minute depending on the pressure your foot is applying on the accelerator.

In a two-cycle or stroke engine the first and second cycles are combined. The third and fourth cycles are combined. The piston in a two-cycle engine is used as a sliding valve for the cylinder intake and exhaust port. The crankcase is used as a pump, in order to slightly compress new fuel/air mixtures and force it into the cylinder cavity.

A mechanic must fully understand how engines work, function and how their application is in order to be able to repair them correctly. A mechanic must know the difference between 2-cycle and 4-cycle engines, as they do sound different. Two-cycle engines are typically small in nature and are used in handy yard and construction applications. They develop their power as a result of high revolutions, whereas four-cycle engines are larger in size delivering many more times of foot-pounds of torque or twisting power to the shaft typically found in automobiles and larger construction equipment and smaller airplanes.

Today's passenger automobiles, pickups, to heavy-duty trucks now and for decades use fuel injectors as their method of combining fuel/air mixtures to each separate cylinder. Carburetors are used on smaller engines that run at a constant speed, carrying a constant load for long periods of time, which can be relatively simple in design because they are only required to mix fuel/air mixture at a constant demand.

Battery ignition systems are found on all internal combustion engines such as those installed on lawn tractors, passenger vehicles, pickups, to light weight trucks. Some diesel powered, passenger vehicles, pickups to super heavy-duty trucks and other industrial vehicles used a modified battery ignition systems to fire glow-plugs during the starting process; then switch to heat of compression to keep the diesel engine running. Diesel engines in trucks, tractors and super heavy-duty equipment are often found left idling for long periods of time. Turn them off and on again several times because of the high battery demands to start diesel engines each time takes place.

Mechanics need to know how to inspect, service and replace batteries. Today's complex automobiles demand so much more from their batteries than older model vehicles. Today's complex automobiles require heavy-duty batteries to start engines, plus supplying electrical power to a number of appliances such as security systems detectors, clocks, and cameras, diodes-lights and monitoring, and regulating onboard computers even when the vehicles are not in use regenerating and recharging the battery. Like a horse these power appliances and items need to be feed by a durable battery that is slowly being drained while the regenerating process is at rest.

Starters in cars must be repaired. Mechanics must know how to repair starters and/or replace them. Electric starters are being used more often. Many cars operate with electricity. Electric starters have a solenoid type, engagement system. A rewind spring is mounted inside the cover of most recoil starters.

Tune-ups are important in the maintenance of a car. The engine should be tuned-up periodically. Normally a mechanic should check the condition of the spark plug wiring, points and condenser. Make the necessary adjustments to the components and the carburetor. Have the motor oil and filter changed. Have the carburetor serviced if needed.

Some steps that mechanics follow in tuning up any 2-cycle engines are: remove the air cleaner and check for the proper servicing. Check the oil level and fill if necessary. Check the fuel line filter if separate from the carburetor. Remove the blower housing and inspect the rope and rewind assembly and starter clutch of the starter mechanism. Thoroughly clean the cooling fins with compressed air, if possible and check that all control flaps operate freely. Spin the flywheel to check compression. It should be spun in direction opposite to normal rotation; and as rapidly as possible. A sharp rebound indicates good compression.

In a 4-cycle engine mechanics may also check compression with a gauge in place of the spark plug. Remove the carburetor and disassemble and inspect it for wear and damage. Wash it in solvent; replace parts as necessary and reassemble. Set the initial adjustments.

Inspect the crossover tube or the intake elbow for damage gaskets.

Remove the flywheel and check for seal leakage, both on the flywheel and power take off sides. Check the flywheel key for wear and tear. Remove the breaker cover and check for proper sealing. Inspect the breaker points and condenser. Replace or clean and adjust them. Check the plunger or the cam. Lubricate the cam followers. Check the coil and inspect all wires for breaks or damaged to the insulation. Be sure the lead wires do not touch the flywheel. Check the stop switch and the wire leads.

Replace the breaker cover, using sealer where the wires enter. Install the flywheel and time the ignition if necessary. Set the air gap and check for ignition spark. Remove the cylinder head, check the gasket, remove the spark plug, clean off the carbon, and inspect the valves for proper seating. Replace the cylinder head, using a new gasket. Torque it to the proper specifications, and set the spark plug gap or replace the plug if necessary.

The mechanic should replace the oil and fuel and check the muffler for restrictions or damage. Then he should adjust the remote control linkage and cable, if used for correct operation. Then the mechanic should service the air cleaner and he should check the gaskets and element for damage. Then the mechanic should run the engine and adjust the idle and high-speed mixture of the carburetor.

If an engine is out of service for more the 30-days, the following steps should be performed. Replenish the existing fuel. Run the engine for 5 to 10 minutes until it is thoroughly warmed up to normal operating temperatures. If you plan to store a gasoline vehicle for more than 90 days, remove all fuel from the engine to protect it from corrosion. Fill the crankcase with clean oil after drawing the old oil out. Remove the spark plug and squirt about an ounce of oil into the cylinder. Coat the engine walls by turning the engine over several times without starting it.

When a car has been in storage for a long period of time, a mechanic should clean or replace the air cleaner. He should clean the governor linkage, making sure that it is in good working order and oil all joints. The mechanic should plug the exhaust outlet and the fuel inlet openings by using clean, lintless rags. Remove the battery and store it in a cool place where there is no danger of freezing. Do not store a wet cell battery directly in contact with the ground or cement floor, as it will establish a ground and discharge itself. Store the battery on a workbench or on blocks of wood placed on the floor. Wipe off or wash the engine. Wash only after the engine has had time to cool off. Coat all parts that might rust with a light coating of oil. Cover the stored care with a protective car cover.

Maintenance of your car is important so you will be safer and be able to drive your car with confidence.

TWENTY-NINE

REINCARNATION

Reincarnation means we are born again and again. We keep the same soul. However, we re-embody into a new body each lifetime. Why do we reincarnate? Our soul needs to experience life on the physical plane. We rest between each life on the astral plane. We need to experience life on the physical dimension to learn lessons here. We also keep learning when we are on the astral plane.

By incarnating, our soul has a chance to evolve step by step. We learn to live by Cosmic Laws. Each lifetime gives us the opportunity to grow and become one with God. We mature and develop usually more and more from lifetime to lifetime.

Reincarnation is a form of recycling. We leave the physical body at death. Our astral body exists within our physical body. Our astral body takes us to the inner planes where we assimilate and digest as well as evaluate what we have learned on the physical plane.

Our soul has an opportunity to be awakened. As our opportunity to be awakened as our soul evolves, we learn how to live by cosmic laws and principles. We should appreciate that reincarnation exists. We live in manvantaras, which are 432,000,000 years in cycle after cycle. Our goal is to overcome obstacles of negative karma (cause and effect) experiences from incarnation to incarnation.

A number of religious groups such as Theosophists, Buddhists, Jews and Metaphysical students learn about reincarnation. Edgar Cayce documented thousands of cases of reincarnation to prove that reincarnation exists. We should be opened minded about the reality that reincarnation exists.

THIRTY

THE SEVEN-FOLD PATH

The spiritual path is a seven-fold path. We live in seven dimensions constantly even though the physical dimension seems to be the main dimension. The seven planes or dimensions are the I Am Presence, Christ Self, Soul presence, mental body, emotional body, astral body and physical body.

We should become aware consciously of the seven bodies mentioned above. Each body is in a dimension. The physical body is apparent to us. The physical eyes do not see the six invisible bodies. Yet, all seven bodies affect us.

The seven-fold path is a special path to follow. Daily meditation can help us become one with our I Am Presence and Christ Self. We need to seek wisdom and knowledge from our higher self or inner presence. By seeking to live by the Will of God we can find ourselves.

The more we look within the more we can understand our permanent reality. This inner reality is merged with our I Am Presence and Christ Self. We become One with God and All good.

The seven-fold path exists in the cosmic plan. The Cosmos is made up of inner dimensions. Our I Am Presence and Christ Self are interconnected with the Great Central Sun. The source of cosmic light emanates from the Great Central Sun, which is an invisible Sun behind the physical Sun.

The Seven-Fold Path is affected by Cosmic Laws such as love, karma, recycling, polarities of positive and negative, correspondences and relativity, magnetism and electromagnetism. We need to learn to live by the seven-fold path.

THIRTY-ONE

THE GOLDEN AGE

We are living in a Golden Age today. Many religions and philosophies have been created through the many centuries. Religions were more advanced within the late nineteenth century, the twentieth and twenty-first century.

The Theosophical Society was established by Madame Helena Blavatsky around 1875. Then the Temple of the People was founded in 1898 by Francia La Due. Madame Helena Blavatsky's co-founder was William Quan Judge. The Theosophical Society spread from New York City, New York to India. Eventually, this Metaphysical society was active in London, England. Many theosophical groups formed in larger cities.

The Temple of the People moved from Syracuse, New York to Halcyon, California in 1903. Francia La Due established the Temple headquarters in Oceano,

California first. Eventually, the Temple headquarters was moved to Halcyon. The Temple of the People building was built in 1922-1923. The William Quan Judge Library and office was built in the early 1930s.

The Theosophical Society is a New Age Movement, which focuses on Ancient Eastern and Western awareness. Reincarnation means, rebirth of the soul in a physical body lifetime after lifetime. Karma, which is cause and effect, also exists.

Until Theosophy was introduced in 1875 reincarnation and karma had not been taught in Christian groups. Buddhism was finally presented in the 20th Century in America. Gautama Buddha introduced an eight-fold path in India many centuries ago. Buddhism has spread around the world during the Golden Age.

The Temple of the People is another New Age Movement. Cosmic laws are taught such as reincarnation karma, correspondences, positive and negative polarities, love, unity, transmutation and purity. The Temple of the People is a Foursquare Movement. More enlightenment has take place in the Temple of the People.

Guy Ballard, who has brought forth New Age teachings, founded the Saint Germain Movement in the early 1930s. Guy Ballard delivered messages from Master Jesus, Master Saint Germain, Archangel Michael and Mother Mary. The same cosmic laws are presented in the St Germain Movement as The Temple of the People.

The Summit Lighthouse was established in 1958. Teachings and messages of Ascended Masters, Saint

Germain, Morya Kuthumi, Hilarion, Dwal Ku, Lord Maitreya, Mother Mary, archangel Michael and Gabriel and others were delivered by Mark and Elizabeth Clare Prophet. These New Age teachings focus on the ascension in the light. Decrees are chanted about transmutation, purity and self-surrender. If 51% of one's karma is dissolved a soul many go to his or her ascension. Flames of freedom negative karma are dissolved.

Other New Age groups have developed through the years. Each group has brought more enlightenment to souls seeking the truth. The Golden Age has been an opportunity for more souls to become awakened and enlightened.

During the Golden Age souls have become accelerated in consciousness. Individuals can expand their awareness. More people are much more open-minded today. More people are seeking deeper truths. Masses of people have more understanding during this Golden Age. If we search for eternal verities we can become much more enlightened.

THIRTY-TWO

SURVIVAL IN THE WILDERNESS

Survival in the wilderness is a challenge. Wildernesses are filled with wild animals, unsettled landscapes and mountains. Generally a person must learn to survive out in isolated, dangerous places many miles from any civilization.

Daniel and Cheryl Tyson took a journey in their jeep out into an isolated region of Australia. They had plenty of gasoline when they began their journey. They traveled for many miles. They expected to refill their jeep along the way. However, there were no gasoline stations once they drove into an irritated desert.

Along the desert terrain, Daniel and Cheryl drove passed tumble weeds and rocky terrain. It was very dry and hot in the desert. Cheryl and Daniel had water jugs stored in the jeep. Daniel and Cheryl had packed their bedrolls, some food and other camping essentials to use on the journey.

Daniel was driving the jeep. He had to drive over rough, rocky terrain in Australia. He was in the Northern Territory. Uluru National Park is in the southern region of the Northern territory. Daniel drove through the Uluru National Park. Ayers Rock is in this national park. In fact, Uluru is the original name given by the Aborigines for Ayers Rock.

Uluru is a massive rock formation in the desolate center of Australia. Ayers Rock is two hundred million years old. This enormous red-orange rock is the largest rock in the world. A six-mile hike takes several hours to walk around. Uluru means "Shadowy Place" and is sacred to the Aborigines.

Daniel and Cheryl hiked around Ayer's Rock. They encountered wild dingoes near the rock. They had to throw rocks at the wild dingoes to scare them away. Daniel and Cheryl explored around this magnificent rock. There were deep curries in the rock walls and some caves at the base of the rock.

It was a warm, sunny day. Daniel and Cheryl stopped to rest. They laid a canvas on the rich red soil and took food out of their backpacks to eat. They had tuna sandwiches with lettuce, tomatoes and pickles with mustard and mayonnaise on rye bread. Once they ate their sandwiches they ate fresh fruit such as apples and bananas. They sipped cold, ice tea from their thermos containers.

After their picnic lunch Daniel and Cheryl cleaned up, rolled up the canvas and continued their hike around Ayers Rock. Some Aborigine, ancient drawings were visible on some of the cave walls that they explored. As they continued walking some Aborigines showed up.

Daniel and Cheryl noticed that the three Aborigines had painted faces. One carried a didgeridoo, which is an ancient blowing instrument. The second Aborigine carried a long spear. The third Aborigine was dressed in homemade skins around their private parts. Their chests, legs and arms were bare. They were barefooted as well.

One of the Aborigines spoke to Daniel and Cheryl in broken English. He said, "Who are you?" Daniel replied, "I am Daniel and this is Cheryl." The Aborigines stared at Daniel and Cheryl without smiling. The same Aborigine spoke, "Why are you here?" Daniel answered, "We are exploring Ayers Rock." The Aborigine said sternly, "You are not allowed to climb up our rock!" Daniel realized that the Aborigine was warning him.

Daniel asked, "Why can't we climb Ayer Rock?" The second Aborigine said, "This is our sacred rock. No one is allowed to climb it!" Cheryl looked at the Aborigines intently. She knew the Aborigines had been in Australia for thousands of years. This was their sacred rock. Cheryl replied, "We will not climb up Ayers' Rock." Daniel responded, "We are only walking around this rock."

Daniel and Cheryl decided to continue on their hike around Ayers Rock. The Aborigine walked away also as Daniel and Cheryl departed from them. They walked back to their jeep and Daniel drove away from Ayers Rock. He headed northeast to Alice Springs.

Alice Springs was a pleasant resort. Daniel and Cheryl camped at the outskirts of this resort. They witnessed hundreds of kangaroos jumping and hopping around. They found out that there are more kangaroos in Australia then people. The little joeys cling to their mothers. They stay in their mother kangaroo's pouch. Cheryl and Daniel observed many kangaroos and how they behaved.

The next day Daniel and Cheryl packed their jeep after breakfast. Daniel drove the jeep with Cheryl at his side as he drove toward Tennant Creek. They saw more kangaroos along the way. They were in the land down under below the equator. They finally arrived at Tennant Creek, which was flowing swiftly. They stopped at the creek to refresh themselves. They took off their shoes and waded through the creek. The creek water was cool and they were able to relax as the water flowed over their bare feet and legs. They also cooled their faces with creek water.

Daniel and Cheryl decided to camp near Tennant Creek. They set up their tent first by pitching wooden stakes. They placed canvas covering and tied the canvas with ropes to hold the tent in place. They placed canvas on the tent floor. Then they unrolled their bedding inside the tent.

Daniel gathered brush and sticks to start a fire. He dug a hole, at least five feet away from the tent and placed brush in the it with sticks arranged in the brush.

Daniel started a campfire. Meanwhile, Cheryl went to the creek to fish. She used a fishing rod, string and fish bate.

After 7 to 8 minutes, a fish bit the fish bate. Cheryl pulled a large trout out of the water. She put it in a bucket of cold water from the creek once it was dead. Cheryl continued to fish for more fish. She brought the fish near the campfire.

Cheryl peeled some potatoes and sliced them up. She placed the potatoes over the campfire. The vegetables were cooking in a pan. Cheryl cleaned and cut the fresh water fish. She placed the fish in another frying pan. She let the fish fry on both sides. The frying fish aroma smelled delicious.

After the food was cooked, Daniel and Cheryl sat down to enjoy their meal. They enjoyed the fresh fish, potatoes and vegetables. Cheryl served some bread, which she took out of the packed containers. For dessert, Daniel and Cheryl ate fresh, washed apples and mangoes. They drank some tea, which they had stored in a thermos container.

After dinner, Cheryl and Daniel cleaned up the utensils. Daniel kept the campfire burning especially when it was dark. The Moon came out. There was a bright moonlight illuminated over Tennant Creek. Wild animals could be heard in the distance. Owls were hooting. Wild animals could be heard moving in the bushes and woods.

Daniel and Cheryl went into their big tent and got into their bedrolls to rest. They received light from the campfire. They listened to the night sounds until they fell asleep. In the middle of the night Daniel woke up suddenly when he felt something crawling on his body.

Daniel jumped up and brushed a long snake off of himself. The blue-green snake slithered away and out of the tent. Daniel went outside the tent. He took a long stick and poked the snake to scare it away. Cheryl woke up and came outside the tent. She saw the snake crawling quickly away.

Cheryl walked over to Daniel and said, "Daniel, are you alright?' Daniel replied, "I'm O.K. A snake was in our tent. I got rid of it." Cheryl said, "Did it hurt you?" Daniel answered, "I was lucky. I don't think it's a poisonous snake. It didn't bite me. "Cheryl responded, "I'm glad the snake didn't bite you."

Daniel warmed his hands at the campfire, which was still simmering. Light was blazing in the campfire with burning embers. Cheryl joined him. She stood by the campfire enjoying the warmth. They both looked up at the Moonlight. Finally, they went back into their tent to rest.

The next morning Daniel and Cheryl packed their jeep with their camping equipment. They continued traveling north in the North Territory. They checked their jeep closely before traveling north. Their four tires appeared in good shape. They continued traveling for many miles. They came to the Tanami Desert. This desert was filled with reddish-brown sand and a few desert plants. The sand was thick, blowing and rippling in the wind.

There were no paved roads in Tanami Desert. Daniel kept driving the jeep in this enormous, dry and hot desert. The sun was piercing down on the desert. Daniel and Cheryl felt the extreme heat and sunlight beating down on them. They were thirsty from the heat.

Cheryl took out the water bag and drank some water to quench her thirst. She handed the water bag to Daniel. He drank some water to quench his thirst.

After Daniel and Cheryl had traveled many miles it became very windy. A sandstorm began. Daniel had to top the jeep because the sand was blowing swiftly. Daniel and Cheryl covered their faces to protect themselves from the blowing sand. The sandstorm continued to rage across the desert. Daniel and Cheryl waited in the their jeep for several hours during the sandstorm.

Finally the sandstorm stopped. Daniel and Cheryl were covered with sand. Their jeep was corroded with sand. Daniel tried to start the jeep but it wouldn't start. The motor and interior parts were covered with sand. The tires were completely covered with sand. The tires were stuck in the sand.

Daniel realized that the jeep was no longer useful to travel in. Daniel and Cheryl were stranded in the desert. They were forced to walk across the desert in the extreme heat. They carried some of their belongings with them so they could camp. They had many miles to travel to come to civilization. Daniel and Cheryl kept tracking in the desert sands. The sand was hot and the climate continued to be very arid and hot especially in the desert. Daniel and Cheryl trudged along one foot after the other. They were hot and became weaker and weaker. Yet, they kept walking north.

Daniel and Cheryl became very sun burned. Their skin became pinkish-red. They began to suffer more and more from the heat exposure. They were worried that they would never come out of the desert alive. It took three days and two nights for the Tysons to cross the desert. They walked passed scorpions and desert snakes moving in the sand.

At last Daniel and Cheryl came to Kakadu National Park. The Aborigine lived in this park. Daniel and Cheryl hoped the Aborigines would accept them. Daniel and Cheryl were glad to be surrounded by greenery and a swamp. They were glad to be in such a beautiful place. Some Aborigines knew that Daniel and Cheryl must have come out of the Tanami Desert.

The Aborigines appeared shy. One of them spoke to Daniel and Cheryl. He said, "Hello. Where have you come from?" Daniel replied, "We have come all the way from Ayers Rock. The Aborigines smiled and said, "You have traveled a long way. Sit down and rest." They were glad to be back in civilization again.

THIRTY-THREE

FORGIVING ENEMIES

We all must deal with enemies during our lifetimes. Enemies can exist in our daily lives in our family, at school, in our neighborhoods and even at church.

How do we know who our enemies are? An enemy attacks its victims. Enemies attempt to harm certain people. They may attempt to destroy individuals who they hate and despise. Enemies must be exposed and stopped before they cause harmful actions to occur.

Enemies must be identified so measures of prevention may take place. We need to learn to forgive our enemies. Some enemies may eventually become friends over a period of time. Other enemies may remain enemies forever.

We need to make an attempt to reverse the tide on our enemies. We need to learn to forgive anyone who attempts to harm us. The law of forgiveness exists.

Forgiveness may heal the problems, which were the causes and effects known as karma.

Jesus, who was an advanced soul, dealt with enemies during his spiritual mission on Earth. In fact, he was crucified because he was rejected by the Sadducees and Pharisees. They persecuted Jesus and accused him falsely of blasphemy and heresy. As a result Jesus suffered on a cross. A crown of thorns was placed on his head pressed down into his scalp to inflict pain and bleeding. Jesus suffered on the cross as he was crucified. Yet, he is said, "Forgive them Lord for they know not what they are doing."

Jesus is known to be a Master today. He had disciples who followed him. Jesus taught humanity to love one another. He said, "We should practice the Golden Rule, which means, Do unto others what you would want done unto yourself." Jesus personally practiced the Golden Rule. He set an example for humanity by treating others with love, kindness and brotherhood.

So, forgive anyone who offends you and who attempts to persecute and harm you. Treat this person like a blood brother or sister. Perhaps, this enemy may change his or her negative attitudes and false judgments about you. Forgive your enemies.

THIRTY-FOUR

HAPPY TIMES

Happy times are special moments and pleasant experiences in our lives. We want to be happy as much as possible. Cheerful, uplifting feelings help us feel good emotionally, physically and spiritually. Happiness is a state of bliss and tranquility.

Joanne Felton wanted to be happy. She grew up in a large family. Her parents were poor and they struggled to make enough to provide for their family. Joanne's mother washed clothes on a washboard. Joanne's father was a janitor part-time.

The Felton's lived in an old, wooden, single floor house. Joanne shared a bedroom with three younger sisters. She was the oldest child out of seven children. Joanne was 16 years old. She had many chores and responsibilities in her family's household. She looked after her younger brothers and sisters on a daily basis. She also washed and dried dishes, mopped floors, vacuumed carpets, dusted furniture, made beds, washed clothes and she even gardened in the yard. Joanne helped her mother with the cooking.

Joanne had little time for relaxing and experiencing pleasures. She tried maintaining a positive attitude despite her situation. Joanne thought about the day when she could have free time to enjoy fun things to do. She wished she could go out to parties, movies and after school activities such as soccer and baseball. Joanne hoped happier times would come soon.

Many months past and Joanne had continued to do many chores and took care of her younger brothers and sisters. Joanne was now 17 years old. She was a junior in high school. She wanted to go to the school dances and her friends' parties. Finally, Joanne spoke to her parents about her desire to enjoy school dances and friends parties.

Mrs. Felton sympathized with her daughter, Joanne. However, she said, "I need your help at home." Joanne looked at her mother with a frustrated expression. She said, "I never have any fun! I'm 17 and I want to go to school dances and to some friends' parties!" Joanne's mother replied, "I'm sorry. But I am swamped around the house. Without you help I cannot manage to keep up!" Joanne responded, "I need some free time like my friends!"

Mrs. Felton looked deeply concerned. She said, "Alright! You can attend your friend's party. When is the party going to take place? Joanne's face lit up. She paused to think of the date of her friend's party. Then Joanne said, "The party is this Saturday night at 7 pm." Mrs. Felton said, "You may go." Joanne replied, "I will need a dress for the party." Joanna's mother answered, "I have no money to give you for a new dress. We are barely paying for food for the family."

Joanne realized that she would have to go to the party in one of her old dresses. She thought about what to wear. Then she decided to make herself a new dress. She looked in a dresser for some fabric. She found some yellow, cotton fabric. It was Wednesday. She had until Saturday to make the new dress.

Mrs. Felton reminded Joanne that she would have to finish all her chores before she went to the party. Joanne tried to spend time sewing her new dress. She picked a dress pattern. She measured the cotton fabric carefully. Then she cut the fabric. She sewed the fabric on an electric sewing machine. The dress was completed by Saturday afternoon. Joanne tried on her new dress. It fit just right. She had a beige coat, which matched the yellow dress.

Joanne completed all her chores on Saturday. She had to clean the house and help prepare meals. After dinner, which was at 5 p.m., Joanne washed and dried the dishes and cleaned up the kitchen and dining room. She went in her bedroom and got in her new dress. She put on here beige coat and she wore white pumps on her feet. Joanne walked to her friend's house, which was down the street in the same block to go to the party. She was excited because she looked forward to this happy occasion.

When Joanne arrived at her friend's house she was warmly greeted as she entered the friend's house. Joanne looked attractive in her new dress. There were refreshments such as cakes, cookies, candies and cold sodas. Music was playing. Joanne visited with her friends. Finally, she was asked to dance. So, she danced with different high school fellows. She was having a good time. She enjoyed the refreshments.

Joanne felt happy because she had a wonderful time at her friend's party. She hoped she would be able to go to the coming school dance several weeks later. She continued to do her chores and looked after her brothers and sisters. She told her mother and father that she wanted to go to the school dance at the high school. They gave their consent because Joanne always completed her chores and babysitting. She had proven that she was very reliable.

The high school dance was on Friday night. Joanne wore the same yellow dress to the dance. She was asked to dance frequently by different fellows at the dance. Joanne was popular. She had a great time. She felt much better because she was given an opportunity to enjoy parties and school dances. She deserved to have happy times in her life.

THIRTY-FIVE

POLICEMEN CAN BE UNFAIR

Police candidates are given special training to become policemen. Some policemen try being objective and fair when dealing with the public. Other policemen are not so objective or fair. Such policemen are less likely to give drivers tickets.

Policemen have the responsibility of upholding the laws. They go in search of suspects who commit crimes such as robberies, murders and vandalism, etc. They arrest suspects and take them to the police stations to be booked and placed in jail.

Some policemen become very harsh and rough with people they suspect. They handcuff their suspects and take them to the police station in their police cars. Suspects must cooperate. It's the law. Policemen wear guns to protect themselves and the public. They enforce the law sometimes by using their guns in the process.

They have to control their suspects in order to take them away safely to the police station.

Suspects are questioned and fingerprinted. Photographs are taken of suspects. These photographs are kept in the suspect's personal file. The police department must keep records of each suspect. The information kept at the police station is used later in court.

Policemen are sworn to protect the public and must obey the law and maintain their moral standards, too. They are not allowed to abuse anyone they pickup as well as people they issue citations to. Some policemen tend to be somewhat abusive and rough if their suspects become difficult to capture and control.

Every policeman should be fair and behave in accordance to the laws in a professional manner. Policemen are needed to help maintain manmade laws. It a policeman is fair and behaves in a professional way the public is likely to respond better.

THIRTY-SIX

THE SUMMER PLACE

Selma and Alex Wilcox had been married ten years. Both of them worked. Selma was an interior decorator and Alex was a successful businessman. The Wilcoxes lived in a beautiful neighborhood in Santa Barbara. Their home was magnificent looking. They lived in a two-story home with five bedrooms.

Selma and Alex enjoyed sitting out in their garden chairs. The sunshine was warm and healing. Their garden was well kept with lovely, colorful flowers, shrubs and evergreen trees. There was a verdant, green lawn, which was mowed regularly.

The Wilcox family enjoyed listening to birds chirping and watched colorful butterflies flying about. Blue jays, robins, sparrows and hummingbirds came into their garden. They had a bird feeder stand. Birds flocked over to the bird feeder stand to pluck birdseeds. The Wilcoxes observed many birds in their garden.

The Wilcoxes were well off. So, they were able to travel to a summer place they had in the woods in Escondido. Their summer cabin was near the beach. Selma and Alex made plans to stay in their summer cabin for their vacation.

When summer arrived the Wilcoxes packed some of their summer clothes and other personal things. They drove to Escondido to their cabin in the woods. When they came to their cabin Alex unlocked the front door of the cabin. Alex and Selma walked into the cabin. They were upset when they saw that their cabin had been vandalized

The cabin furniture was knocked over. The floors were stained and things were lying all over the place. Even the bed in the bedroom was messed up. Alex and Selma were very concerned about the condition of their summer cabin. They had come here to relax and rest. Now they were forced to clean up and straighten out their cabin.

Alex and Selma spent many hours cleaning up their cabin. They were exhausted from spending the time cleaning and straightening out their cabin. They laid down in the double bed to recuperate from working so hard. They went to bed early that evening because they were so tired.

The next morning Selma woke-up first. She heard birds chirping in the distance. Selma decided to prepare breakfast for her husband and herself. She gathered wood to burn in the potbelly stove there in the kitchen. Once the wood was burning, she began preparing breakfast. She had brought some eggs, bacon, bread, butter, jelly, coffee and hash browns, which were stored in a miniature, electric refrigerator. Selma cracked open raw eggs into a frying pan and allowed them to cook and sizzle on the stovetop as she finished scrambling the four eggs. Selma then fried strips of bacon. She put bread in a toaster and then she prepared hot coffee.

Alex woke-up when he smelled breakfast food aromas spreading about the cabin. Alex got out of bed. He put on his bathrobe over his pajamas. He walked into the kitchen. Selma was nearly finished preparing breakfast. Alex smiled and said, "Breakfast is nearly ready."

Selma brought scrambled eggs, bacon and toast to Alex who was seated at the corner table in the kitchen. She already had set the table for two. Napkins were neatly folded. Alex sat down where the plate of food was served. Selma asked, "Would you like some coffee?" Alex answered, "Sure, I'm still wakening up. Coffee will really wake me up!"

Once Selma had all the breakfast food on the table and she had poured coffee for both of them she sat down to join Alex for breakfast. They began eating their breakfast. They were hungry. Breakfast tasted delicious. Alex said, "Thanks for preparing breakfast. It is delicious." Selma replied, "I am glad you are enjoying breakfast." They continued to eat their breakfast.

Alex and Selma looked outside through a nearby window. They saw evergreen trees outside in a nearby grove. After breakfast Selma washed the dishes, cleaned up the kitchen and wiped off the table where the Wilcoxes ate breakfast. Then she dressed in comfortable street clothes. Alex changed into his clothes after taking a bath in a porcelain tub.

It was a sunny day. Alex and Selma walked outside to enjoy looking around. They came to an evergreen grove. The grove smelled fragrant with evergreen leaves, grass and wild berries. Selma and Alex noticed some squirrels scampering around under the trees. Some of the squirrels climbed up trees. Their tails were long and bushy. Some squirrels saw Alex and Selma coming into the grove. They scurried away out of fear. Selma hoped the squirrels would have stayed. There were some wild, brown hares hopping around in the distance. They nibbled on grass and wild flowers.

Selma and Alex walked around in the grove. They observed the sun gleaming through the evergreen trees. The wild flowers were interesting and colorful. The wild hares ran away as Selma and Alex came closer. Then they saw a doe and her two fawns in the distance. The deer were nibbling on grass and evergreen leaves. They remained where they were until Selma and Alex came very close to them. The mother doe made an alerting sound to her fawns. The fawns were spotted. The deer ran away as soon as Selma and Alex came closer to them.

The beach was inviting in Escondido. Alex and Selma walked three blocks down to this pristine beach. They had changed into bathing suits. They brought towels. They wore rubber tabee shoes. Once they approached the beach they went walking near the ocean. They felt ocean water ripple over their feet. The rhythm of the ocean could be felt as they walked on the wet sand.

The ocean felt cold as Alex and Selma walked deeper into it. Waves splashed over them as they walked further and further into the ocean. They began swimming and floating in the ocean. It took awhile to get used of the ocean because it was so cold. Once they adjusted to the cold water, they swam around more freely. Swimming was good exercise for both of them.

Alex began splashing ocean water on Selma in a playful manner. She splashed ocean water back on him Selma kept swimming in deeper waters She swam further out into the ocean. At first she was doing alright. However, several enormous waves splashed over her. She nearly conked out because of the swift ocean waves. Selma suddenly sunk into the deep ocean and disappeared.

Alex became worried when he couldn't see Selma above the ocean water. He swam over to where she had been swimming. Selma was nowhere in sight. Alex decided to swim deeper into ocean water to find Selma. He kept searching for her. Finally, after several minutes, Alex finally located Selma who was sinking deeper into the ocean. She was unable to come to the ocean's surface because she had been sucked into an ocean water, tide pool.

Fortunately, Alex was able to grab Selma and bring her up to the ocean's surface. Selma had almost drowned in the ocean. Alex swam to shore with her on his back. He used CPR methods to help her breathe. Ocean water come out of her mouth onto the beach sand after he used certain CPR techniques to revive her.

When Selma came to and began breathing properly she became conscious again. She was lying on the beach. She looked at Alex. She asked, "What happened?" Alex replied, "You almost drowned in the ocean. I got you out of the ocean just in time! You had a lot of ocean water in your lungs. You have coughed out ocean water from your lungs. Thank goodness! I thought I had lost you!"

Selma began to cry. She realized that she had almost drowned. She was grateful to still be alive. Alex waited on the beach with Selma while she rested to regain enough strength to walk again.

Alex assisted Selma back to the summer cabin. She laid down on their double bed to rest and become restored from her near death experience. Alex ordered food to go from a Chinese restaurant to be delivered at their summer cabin. Alex and Selma ate egg-fu-young, chicken chow mien, pork chop suey, white rice and had fortune cookies for dessert.

Selma's fortune message stated, "You will live a long life and have many adventures." Alex's fortune message stated, "Prosperity will come your way." Alex said, "Both of our fortune messages are good ones! I hope we don't encounter anymore dangers!" Selma replied, "I hope we will be safe. We came here to rest and have fun." Selma and Alex stayed in their summer cabin several more weeks.

THIRTY-SEVEN

BECOMING A WELL KNOWN WRITER

Becoming a writer can be a blessing. Creative imagination takes place when a writer expresses words and ideas on paper. A writer uses descriptive words to develop word pictures—visual images of people, places, things and events.

There are many writing styles used to communicate about topics and issues. A writer should let his or her imagination soar. Many ideas and examples can be freely expressed. A writer may develop novels, nonfiction books, poetry, short stories, articles, diaries, reports, and theses.

To become a well known, successful writer you must use marketing techniques. A writer's books should be distributed at notable, national bookstores, newsstands, book exhibits, community book clubs, and book signing events. A writer can advertise on the Internet as well.

It is helpful to present a writer's books on television talk shows to promote to as many people as possible. The more a writer's books are circulated and sold, the better chance the writer has to become well known. It may take years to become well known as a writer. Some writers become well known sooner than other writers.

Current topics and issues help a new book become more timely and popular to read by many people. Writing techniques, striking book covers, effective synopses and information known as an author's biography adds to the book so people will select the book.

Writers should present their books at different community groups such as the Women's Club, Elks Lodge, Christian Women's Club, AARP, Rotary Club and other groups. Writers need to present their books at conferences, seminars and conventions and at churches and schools.

There are well known writers such as Louisa May Alcott, Ralph Waldo Emerson, Mark Twain, Emily Barrett Browning, Tennessee Williams, Shakespeare, Keats, Shelley and many, many more writers. These writers became well known over the years because their books were distributed and read at schools and sold in many bookstores across the nation. It may be difficult for some writers to become well known. Perseverance, determination and effective selling techniques make a big difference in selling books.

THIRTY-EIGHT

URSULA'S LIFE IN BROOKFIELD

Ursula Atkins lived in Brookfield, Michigan where posies, shrubs, aspen and birch trees grew abundantly. Ursula often walked in meadows where wild flowers were blowing in the wind. Maribells, lupines and wild primroses were growing everywhere. Ursula sniffed the wild flowers and enjoyed the refreshing breeze. Ursula sat down in a meadow and felt the warm sun on her face. She felt at peace in this blissful setting.

Ursula remained seated in the meadow for several hours basking in the sunshine. Clouds formed into dark ones. Soon it began raining lightly at first. Then skies darkened as it began pouring in torrents. Ursula stood up and ran for cover beneath some protective branches laced with dense leaves. The trees provided shelter from the rain. It continued raining heavily for sometime. Ursula waited under the trees, which were like protective umbrellas.

Finally the rain stopped. So, Ursula walked back to her cottage, which was nearby in the woods. Ursula lived in a charming cottage with interesting wood shingles and quaint beige walls. The old, English furniture was exquisite. The cottage had only one bedroom. The bedroom was furnished with a double bed, several dressers and a large mirror. A small walk-in closet was in one corner of the bedroom.

Ursula had a spinet piano, which stood against the wall opposite framed English windows. Ursula sat at her rectangular piano and played some Mazurkas by Frederick Chopin. She was able to play piano pieces by memory. Ursula enjoyed playing the piano. When she was done playing five piano pieces she looked out of the living room windows and noticed it was still raining.

Painting scenic views of the ocean and landscapes was another experience that Ursula enjoyed. She was an excellent artist. Ursula could paint watercolor scenes and oil color scenes. She had extra art canvasses, water colors, oils and a variety of paint brushes available to use when she wanted to paint.

The next day the rain had stopped. The sun was shining. Raindrops were still on leaves, grass and flowers. The raindrops were sparkling. The air was fragrant especially after the rain. Ursula decided to sketch a nature scene. She took a canvass outside and placed it on her easel. She brought a variety of oil colors to paint with.

Ursula placed her easel in an appropriate location in her backyard. She was able to look at a scenic view of a colorful meadow nearby. Ursula took an art pencil and began to sketch the scenic meadow. She began painting the foreground. She continued to paint the colorful meadow. She used bright colors for the wild flowers. Ursula continued painting several hours until she had completed the painting.

The painting looked realistic and colorful. Ursula was pleased with her creative results. Ursula continued to paint more pictures. She took them to an art gallery to have them appraised and put up for sale.

Ursula also was a high school art teacher. She had taught art for twelve years. She had taught many students how to paint scenic views, landscapes, portraits and still life scenes. Ursula was an excellent Art teacher. Many of her students admired and respected her as their Art teacher.

Ursula was thirty-six years old, tall, slender, yet, plain looking. Ursula had never been married. She had lived in her cottage twelve-in-a-half years by herself. She was used to living alone. No man had every approached her about a romantic relationship for many years. She felt homely.

When Ursula was 21 years old she had met a young man with whom she had fallen in love with. She dated a young man, known as Andrew Miller. Andrew was very bright as well as a handsome, young man. He was majoring in the medical field to become a doctor. Ursula dated Andrew for approximately two years. Then Andrew graduated from the university they both were attending. He went away to Medical School in New York City. Ursula never saw Andrew again.

Ursula received a B.A. in Art when she was 23 ½ years old. She began to teach Art when she was 24 years old. She was busy teaching in the small town where she lived. She wasn't able to meet eligible bachelors. Life in Brookfield was slow and quiet. She continued to be productive as an artist and musician.

THIRTY-NINE

AFRAID OF THE DARK

Many people are afraid of the dark. At night if the electricity is off a person's house becomes very dark. Candles and flashlights are used so these individuals can see as they walk around the house.

Dark alleys and dark, narrow streets can be frightening to be in on dark nights when streetlights are out. It is even dangerous to wander around in the dark in streets and alleyways.

Most people keep large flashlights and a lot of candles available in case it becomes dark. Electricity can be turned off unexpectedly. People should prepare for blackouts. Unprepared people become victimized and unable to adjust to the dark.

Shirley Macgregor lived in a three-story house in Los Gatos, California. This house was out in the country isolated from other country homes. Her house was surrounded with large acreages of land, some gardens and surrounding groves. Shirley lived in this enormous house with her Uncle Jeffrey Harris and his wife, Margaret Harris.

During the daytime the three-story house appeared normal with plenty of sunlight beaming in through the windows. Most of the 20 rooms were sunny during the daytime. Shirley felt fairly comfortable living in this big house. However, she was 15 years old. She had no kids her age to play with. She felt lonely and isolated away from people.

Shirley had lived with her parents from her birth to age 14 ½ years old. One day her parents were killed in an airplane crash when they were coming home on an air flight to where they lived. Shirley was staying with neighbors when this tragedy occurred. Now, she was living with her aunt and uncle, who were her closest guardian relatives.

One night Mr. and Mrs. Harris went out to a local concert. It was a school night. So Shirley stayed home to do homework. She was old enough to be on her own at age fifteen. The Harris's planned to be home by 10:30 p.m. that Wednesday night.

After the Harris's left to go to their community concert, Shirley sat in the living room. She did her homework on a coffee table near a large couch. She had turned on several lamps to light up the living room. She even had turned on hallway light so she could go easily to other rooms.

At about 8:42 p.m. suddenly all the electricity went off in the big house. Shirley was sitting in the dark alone. Shirley was frightened because it was so dark. She had not expected this to happen. She had not prepared for this to happen. She had no flashlights available or candles nearby to easily light either.

Shirley became somewhat panicky in the dark. She decided to try to find the kitchen so she could locate some candles or flashlights. She struggled to get across the large living room. She finally found the kitchen. She tripped and fell. Scared as she was, she had difficultly but continued searching for any candles or flashlights. She finally found some candles in the kitchen drawer near the stove.

Shirley had to find some matches in order to light the candles. Shirley suddenly remembered that somewhere nearby there were kerosene lamps in the house, also. After what seemed to be a long search, she found some matches. She found several candles near the matches. She took out several candles. She attempted to light each candle. She finally got one candle lit. The she was able light another candle.

The kitchen was lit up. Shirley was able to see again. She looked for the kerosene lanterns. Two kerosene lanterns were on the shelf in the laundry room. Shirley found the kerosene lamp oil at last. She took the kerosene lamps off of the shelf. The kitchen lit up considerably.

Shirley felt better now that she had enough light. She carried the kerosene lamps into the living room and she placed them in a central location. Shirley sat down to relax and to unwind from the fear she had experienced. It was about 10:30 p.m. The Harris's had not arrived home yet. Shirley waited wishing that they would be home soon. It turned 11:00 p.m. The Harris's still were not home. Shirley became worried that something might have happened to them. At 12:10 p.m. the Harris's finally arrived home. The electricity was still off in the three-story house. They noticed that the front porch light was not on. They had noticed other houses were also dark as they were driving home.

The Harris's had attended a concert in another town, which was fifteen miles beyond the town they lived in. The electricity was on in that town. They had a flat tire on the way home. They stopped to change their flat tire. This took some time. They were lucky that someone came along and helped them change their tire.

When the Harris's came into the house Shirley was relieved to see them. She asked them why they were so late in coming home. Mr. Harris said, "They had a flat tire on the way home. Shirley was glad her aunt and uncle were home again. She felt more secure now that they were there. She didn't like being in the dark. Shirley had found flashlights. She kept the flashlights near her in case of future blackouts.

FORTY

CHANGING WEATHER

Changing weather affects the planet Earth. The Northern Hemisphere is above the equator. The weather becomes very cold during winter, early spring and late autumn. The upper, northern, American states including Alaska plus other countries such as Canada, Greenland, Iceland, Finland, Norway, Sweden, Switzerland, Austria, Russia, Baltic States, China, and other upper northern countries in Europe are located in a much colder climate.

Below the equator and at the Mediterranean Sea are countries in much warmer climates. Tropical, humid weather exists in Africa, Indonesia, and the South Sea Polynesian Islands, Micronesia, Australia, New Zealand, Tasmania and Philippine Islands. There are typhoons, which rage in the tropical zones.

Cyclones occur in the Northern Hemisphere in a dryer climate. The Midwestern States in America are places where cyclones take place unexpectedly. Dust storms whirl up in the sky and the immerging cyclone moves around picking up to great speeds enough to destroy houses, cars, gardens and whole towns.

Heavy rainstorms take place especially during winter months through early spring. It rains a lot in the northern coastal states of Oregon and Washington in America. Alaska has constant changing climates. Eight months it is wintertime in Alaska. There is snow, sleet and ice, which covers the landscape of Alaska, Canada, Greenland, Iceland and the North Pole.

Pleasant climate usually occurs in the western continental 48 states of America during spring, summer and autumn. The southern states of America become very hot during late spring, into summer and part of autumn.

Tropical climates are generally humid and hot most of the year in Africa, Indonesia, the Philippine Islands, Micronesia Australia, New Zealand, Tasmania and southern regions of South America. Climates continue to change during each season.

FORTY-ONE

FLOWERS GROW IN UNUSUAL PLACES

Some wild flowers grow in unusual places in the world. Wild flowers grow on high mountain slopes and ledges. Flowers grow in very cold places in Iceland, Alaska, Canada, Sweden, Norway and Finland. Flowers grow in remote meadows and verdant valleys.

Flowers even grow in tundra country and in snowy landscapes during the spring when the snow begins to melt. Flowers quite often grow in tropical climates. Orchids, birds of paradise, African Violets and many other flowers multiply and spread to many tropical places many miles from where they first grew. Birds are said to responsible for ingesting seeds and spreading them off into distant areas through their droppings.

Flowers continue to grow and thrive in unusual places and climates. They grow in unusual places such as caves, near swamps in swamps and even in deserts.

Lotus flowers grow in ponds. Some flowers grow all year while other flowers grow during given seasons.

Irises, poppies, lilies, gladiolas, nastersums, pansies, daisies, roses, chrysanthemums, geraniums and corcasses grow in the northern hemisphere. Orchids and African violets grow in extremely cold climates. Flowers grow all over the world to add color, aromas and beauty to the Earth. We should cultivate and grow more flowers in our yards, parks and other places to promote the continuation of flowers everywhere. Flowers even grow in cement patios and sidewalk cracks.

Birds and insects such as bees depend on nourishment from flowers. Bees gather pollen and help to pollinate the various plant species from flowers to trees. Birds feed on nectar from flowers. Without flowers our planet Earth would not be beautiful. So, plant flowers in your yards in your gardens. Keep the Earth smelling and looking beautiful.

FORTY-TWO

EXPRESS YOURSELF

Express yourself openly and freely. Self-expression is the best way to communicate effectively. We need to express our thoughts and feelings. Individuals have a right to communicate their opinions and viewpoints directly and candidly.

Different ways to express oneself are communications in discussion groups, presentations, speeches, debates, or personal conversations. Interactions in group discussions can be a dynamic experience for those who respond and interact. Many ideas and thoughts are expressed in groups about many subjects, topics and issues.

Individuals who express their ideas, opinions and viewpoints are usually happier and more socially, adjusted people. Self-expression may lead to free-lance writing, descriptive writing, poems, novels and nonfiction books.

People who express themselves well usually act well on stage, in plays, movies and video presentation. Projection of one's voice, vocal expressions and vocal intonations commands stage presence, which is important in acting.

Pros and cons in debates are presented in speech classes, law courses and in community activities. The pros are the positive viewpoints about issues and topics. Cons are the negative viewpoints expressed about issues and topics.

Self-expression is healthy and is a worthwhile way to communicate with others. We need to express our deepest thoughts. Spouses who communicate effectively with one another are usually better adjusted socially and emotionally. Teachers need to express themselves effectively in order to be excellent educators. Lawyers need to communicate well to present evidence and to present conclusions about different cases.

So, express yourself fluently and effectively so you can be successful socially and economically in the world.

FORTY-THREE

CHILDREN IMITATE THEIR PARENTS

Children imitate their parents. A child learns everything from its parents. A toddler learns simple words step-by-step from his or hers parents. A toddler learns to walk with the encouragement of his or her parents.

Many children become like their parents with certain personality characteristics. A child may develop habits based on the influences of his or her parents. Certain foods are eaten on a daily basis. Ways of cleaning the family home take place Different interests and hobbies may be acquired such as ping-pong, playing games and doing yard work.

Parents speak a certain way with a certain style. Slang words and certain dialects are learned during childhood. Beliefs and attitudes are developed in the home. Parents generally communicate their religious beliefs, feelings, opinions and attitudes to their children.

It is important for parents to teach their children about worthwhile values and laws of society. Children must learn to behave in acceptable, social ways. Children are taught what is right and wrong at home, from the community and the world. Children learn from their elders and other children how to relate to one another.

Children generally do better in school if they have been provided with a stimulating, educational environment in their homes. Parents should provide cultural experiences, books, art, gardens and communication skills to help their children grow and develop socially, emotionally and mentally.

Children who are provided with a stimulating home environment and have educated parents usually become well educated themselves and carry on traditions with professional careers and occupations. So, parents need to set an example and be effective teachers as well as friends to their children.

FORTY-FOUR

MADONNA INN

Madonna Inn is located in San Luis Obispo, California. Madonna Inn was created and built by Alex Madonna in 1956. Madonna Inn has several dining rooms, a coffee shop and a first class restaurant. This inn is famous for its bakery. Pies and cakes are baked Bavarian, German and Swiss styles. Cream pies are very delicious. It is one of the central coast's top, local and tourist destination and is known worldwide for its reputation of elegance, service and beauty.

The main dining room is lavishly decorated with angels, grape vines, stained glass windows, fancy wallpaper and well decorated tables. There is an attractive, wooden dance floor that many patrons love to dance with their very own special someone under the mood lighting that enhances their partner's image. They have their regular house, dance band that entertains and delights their patrons nightly. Madonna Inn is a Mecca for the traveling, vacationing tourist and visitors who love and enjoy eating and dining out. The food is elegantly prepared and is served by gracious and caring attendants. Cocktails and regional, famous, recognized wines are featured from their amply stocked and beautifully appointed, beverage bar.

During Thanksgiving and Christmas holiday seasons, the Madonna Inn is beautifully transformed by staff who painstakingly place every decoration just so to enhance the Inn's festive seasonal appearances. Santa Claus is seen in his slay. Angel's images are placed everywhere. Illuminated Christmas trees colorfully decorated are placed throughout the Madonna Inn.

The coffee shop is where locals and tourists come to eat breakfast or simply sip coffee. Family and friends have a tasty treat. The coffee shop is beautifully decorated with mural paintings, tiffany lamps, stained glass window treatments and plush floor coverings. The coffee shop includes the well-known bakery where delicious cream and fruit pies are baked daily. German Bavarian cake is served; but nothing tops their seven layered "mile high" chocolate cake decorated with curled chocolate strips that is simply a customer's favorite, decadent dessert ordered by many a patron.

Breakfast, lunch and dinner are served in the coffee shop. Steaks, lamb, chicken and fish entrées are served in the main dining room. Sandwiches and salads complete meals as well as elegant desserts, which are served with a touch of elegance in the coffee shop, too.

Madonna Inn is well known for its tourist attractions for its unique and elegant, motel rooms. Each room is individually decorated with a theme in mind and given a name that expresses the décor. Well known statesman, famous entertainers and world travelers make the motel a favorite destination stop. Honeymooners enjoy staying in these unique honeymooner suites. For locals, it's a special get-away, weekend, vacation stop where they can enjoy the ambiance and elegance without the distant travel, mileage barrier here at the Madonna Inn in San Luis Obispo, California. It's a must-see location.

FORTY-FIVE

SWIMMING IN A PUBLIC POOL

Public swimming pools exist in most cities and larger towns. Chlorine is generally put in public pools to purify and disinfect pool water from harmful germs. It is important to clean public pools regularly so people will be safe and remain healthier. Too much chlorine may cause a burning sensation in swimmer's eyes. Use of over the counter treatments such as Visine will clear redness and irritation from your eyes.

Swimming races take place at public pools. These swimming races take place regularly. The pool is measured so swimmers line up to swim across the pool in their teams. The winners are swimmers who are able to swim across the pool and back in the shortest amount of time.

Swimmers have the opportunity to go swimming regularly in public swimming pools. Professional swimmers practice swimming and exercising in public pools. Swimming coaches and instructors work with swimmers to prepare them for swimming races and contests. There are swimming drills during instruction time. Daily and weekly coaching help strengthen young swimmers prepare them for swimming matches.

The general public goes to public swimming pools during specific hours on a daily basis. The general public enjoys having an opportunity to go swimming in heated pools that are cleaned out and treated regularly.

Some public pools are very large. Motel and hotel pools are not as large, Public schools, high schools and colleges have large pools. Every pubic pool must be cleaned out and the water be tested for chorine purification.

It is safer to swim in public pools than in the ocean. Ocean water may be polluted. Rough waves can suck a person into the undertoes in the ocean. Lifeguards guard public pools. So, swim in a public swimming pool for safety reasons.

FORTY-SIX

AWAKEN TO GOD

God is everywhere and in everything. God is an invisible, intelligent life force, which promotes new life and protects all living things. God is infinite and all knowing; God is very intelligent and protects all life forms constantly.

God created the Cosmos with stars and planets revolving in solar systems. Human beings were created by God in His likeness to live on the Earth to dominate over all living Earthly creatures in peace and harmony. Human beings have been endowed with the intelligence and they have the ability to think, reason and have feelings. Human beings were made in God's image. We have the potential to become like God if we develop our God-like spirituality within us.

Each soul has a blueprint of God's inner wisdom stored within us and every soul is to awaken to God's higher consciousness. Higher conscious is the way and the light to God's Kingdoms. There are inner dimensions within the Cosmos. These inner dimensions are part of God's reality. One dimension interconnects with other dimensions. An awakened soul is able to realize inner dimensions.

So, awaken to God awareness and enlightenment. Become fulfilled with God's awareness. You will be happier and experience deeper consciousness.

FORTY-SEVEN

AMERICAN PROPAGANDA

America has developed an image around the world. Americans are known to be warlike and aggressive. Americans have fought wars in Korea, Vietnam, Iraq, Afghanistan and other places. Our American presidents have been concerned about problems in other places in the world hoping to help settle long-standing conflicts.

People in different countries have certain attitudes about Americans. Many people have communicated untrue propaganda about Americans. Much of the propaganda is slander. Untrue, malicious statements have been made and are being said about Americans.

It is true that our American soldiers have been sent overseas to the Middle East to fight against terrorism. America was attacked September 11, 2001. More than 3,000 innocent civilians were killed and many others injured in New York City that day. So, American soldiers were sent overseas to fight against terrorists and to end terrorism.

The truth is that Americans want to live in peace, harmony and prosperity. Petroleum oil products must be imported from the Middle East because at one time long ago it was far easier and cheaper to do this than exploring and test drilling domestically. The American oil companies find it difficult to battle against the various, domestic, environmental groups who declare all kinds of unsubstantiated bogus claims as to the dangers of oil extraction and processing may cause the environment to become polluted.

While there may be some violations, most oil companies act responsibly to protect the environment and life in the Middle East. Such environmental impact restrictions are considerably less harsh or nonexistent and thus the cost of extraction and providing petroleum products is substantially less there for the American refineries to buy in the Middle East and have it shipped here for refining. Americans depend on cheap oil and gas to drive their cars. We should ask our government to ease up on some of our own environmental regulations allowing the locating of natural resources to become easier and more affordable for the American public to drill for oil and produce the by-products including gasoline at a cheaper price for our vehicles.

The United Nations is located on American soil in New York City. Americans should abide by the philosophy of the United Nations. We should promote peace and good will around the world. We will be able to change the negative propaganda that has maliciously spread around the world about Americans.

Negative propaganda can be harmful and very malicious. Avoid creating propaganda that can only damage America's image around the world. This is not to say other foreign governments and hugh international business entities also have their own disinformation propaganda machinery working over time to tarnish images and reputations of others hoping to improve their own lot in the world court of opinion.

FORTY-EIGHT

VIETNAM TRAGEDY

The war in Vietnam turned out to be a tragedy because many Vietnamese people and American soldiers were killed during battles and bombings. The Americans fought against communism and terrorism takeover in Vietnam. These veterans came home to criticism by many who didn't understand purpose and cruelty of the war at the time. Americans are just beginning to learn what terrorism is really all about. America's finest men and women continue fighting to eliminate the threat of terrorism around the world.

Communism had spread in Asia and the Soviet Union. Communism means the government owns the land and public buildings and dwelling places. The communist government dictates what the people can and cannot do. There are many restrictions so that the people are not free to make many decisions on their own like selecting their own occupation, religious beliefs or home sites. The Communist régime controls nearly every move they made plus the money supply received by the people.

The American government believes in freedom of speech, freedom of occupations and freedom of religion. As a result American presidents, and Congress opposed communism. They have fought against communist take-over in upper Europe, in parts of Asia and other countries. Communists have taken over in many places for many years.

Americans were unable to win the war against communist take-over in Vietnam. Because of this the Vietnamese people continued to be controlled by the Chinese Communist. The tragedy of many American soldiers being killed during battles in Vietnam has not been forgotten. Many Americans opposed this war in Vietnam, which also caused a lot of money to be spent. Vietnam is still controlled by the Chinese Communist Government today.

FORTY-NINE

WEARING GLASSES

Wearing glasses may be a necessity for some people. Once one's eyes are examined an optometrist is able to determine whether a person needs to wear glasses. They also can evaluate your eyes as to whether you have pending eye disease and they can perform eye surgery.

Some people are nearsighted. Other people are farsighted. Some people only need to wear glasses to read. Many people wear dark glasses outdoors to avoid the glaring, sun damage. Others just want to look cool in ultra-violet, dark glasses for most protective, harmful lighting.

Many people wear glasses. There are many kinds of glasses. Some glasses have dark, thick rims. Other glasses have light, wire thin rims. Thicker lenses are placed in the center of both glass sections. Some glasses are very colorful while other glasses are very plain without colors. The intensity and thickness of lenses vary.

Anyone who wears glasses should have protective cases in order to shield glasses from scratches when they are not being used. Cases can be soft, colorful, vinyl to velvet lined, hard plastic cases in basic colors.

There are individuals who do not want to wear glasses. They think glasses are unattractive to wear. They prefer to wear contact lenses. Contact lenses are not comfortable to wear. Sometimes contact lenses fall out and get lost or ruined. It is best to wear glasses to protect one's eyes. Many glasses today are attractive to wear.

Dark glasses are interesting to look at. There are many shapes as well as glass coloring produced. People look exotic in dark glasses. Even movie stars look good with different, dark glasses on.

Wearing glasses to see better is very acceptable as well as necessary. Many people need to wear glasses every day. They take their glasses off when they go to bed to protect them. So, if you need to wear corrective glasses don't hesitate to wear them.

FIFTY

HOW TO BECOME A FAMOUS PAINTER

Painters need to present their paintings at Art exhibits, Art Galleries and at special locations out in the open. More people have a chance to view an artist's paintings when the paintings are distributed in many locations.

Some painters take their paintings to workshops, art seminars and to art festivals. Some paintings are displayed in churches, public schools and public libraries. If a professional painter teaches art classes and workshops his or her paintings may become better known.

Well-known artists usually have been painting for years. Their artwork has been distributed to many art galleries, museums and public places where they can be seen and sold. Paintings can be filmed in art documentaries to be presented to the public.

Individuals can aspire to become well known artists. They can also advertise in art magazines, newspapers and in brochures about their art productions. Different styles of painting may become famous, unique styles of art. Painters experiment with colors shapes, perspectives and brush strokes when they paint.

Some painters are well known for using oil paints. They may paint landscapes, still life, existential designs and portraits. A given, art technique may be applied. Vincent Van Gogh became famous because he used bright colors, which was not usually the style during his generation. Rembrandt became known for portrait paintings. Reuben became known for lily pond paintings and garden scenes. Paul Reynolds is known for oil paintings of cottage and garden scenes.

Well known painters are appreciated for their artistic techniques and artistic talents for unique painting styles.

FIFTY-ONE

THE WILL TO LIVE

The will to live is important. No matter how ill a person can become he or she should have a purpose for living to overcome hardships and challenges.

Henry Lowe was quite ill with pneumonia. He could hardly breathe. Henry was in the hospital in the intensive care unit. He had tubes up his nose. A large, oxygen container was near his hospital bed.

Several visitors came to see Henry. One of them was his sister, Jean and the other visitor was his Uncle Joe. Jean and Uncle Joe came in one at a time to visit with Henry. Jean came in first to see Henry. Jean looked at Henry with expression sadness, concern and worry. Henry's eyes were closed and he was breathing very heavily. Jean decided to speak to Henry in hopes that he would respond to her. She said, "Hello Henry. How are you?"

Henry didn't respond at first. Jean spoke again. "Henry, I am here to visit with you. It's Jean." Henry opened his eyes slowly. He was still breathing heavily. Henry looked at Jean. He finally spoke to her. He said, "Jean, hi." Jean continued, "I hope you will get well soon." Henry stared at Jean. He appeared downcast and seriously ill. He replied, "I have pneumonia. I feel awful." Jean responded, "I hope the doctor has given you antibiotics for pneumonia." Henry replied, "The doctors and nurses have given me different antibiotics. I feel very drained."

Jean looked at Henry with more concern. She said, "Henry, don't give up. You can get over pneumonia. Have faith in God. I will pray for you." Henry looked up at Jean. He thought about what she had said. Jean said, "I'll come to see you again soon." Jean said goodbye and she left the intensive care room.

Henry continued to breathe heavily. Uncle Joe came into the intensive care room after Jean left. He walked over to Henry's hospital bed. He noticed how pale and tired looking Henry was. He said, 'Howdy Henry. "How are they treating you?" Henry glanced at Uncle Joe. He replied, "O.K. I don't feel well at all." Uncle Joe said, "I heard you have pneumonia. You can lick this disease. Hang in there." Henry knew his uncle was trying to encourage him to get well.

After Uncle Joe left Henry, he laid in his hospital bed. He thought about what Jean and his uncle had said to him when they came to visit him. He realized that he must have faith and hope in order to get well. He needed to have the will to live.

Several weeks went by day by day. Henry stayed in the hospital. His name was put in healing bowls at churches in the area. More friends and relatives came to visit with Henry. He gradually began to recover from pneumonia. Finally, after three and half weeks he recovered from this disease.

Henry was very glad to recover from pneumonia. When he first came down with this dreaded disease he thought he wouldn't get well again. With the encouragement from his friends and relatives, Henry became well. Prayers said over and over by others helped him get well. Henry was glad to be alive.

FIFTY-TWO

DINING OUT

Dining out can be an exciting experience. There are many interesting restaurants to dine in. Many people like to eat out in order to relax and have different foods at exotic places. There are restaurants for seafood, Italian, Chinese, Hindu-Indian, German, or Korean food. They could eat Creole, Russian or American food. Each restaurant is decorated with a special decor. Waiters and waitresses dressed in specific clothes for their jobs. Prices varied at each restaurant, café and bistro. Fast food is generally less expensive.

Sheldon O'Connor and Suzette O'Connor liked to dine out frequently. They both were retired and their children were grown up and out of their family home. So, they selected different restaurant and diners to eat at every week. Sheldon chose a Thai restaurant to dine at.

They lived in San Francisco so they had a wide selection of quality restaurants to choose from.

Suzette and Sheldon drove to the Thai Restaurant across town. It was exotic looking and intriguing to look at. They walked into this Thai diner and were greeted by a hostess near the entrance. She was dressed in a Thai costume and her hair was elegantly styled. The hostess took the O'Connors to a table near a big window. When they were seated they were given menus. Sheldon and Suzette studied the minus.

The O'Connors ordered Thai chicken rice, Thai vegetables and leafy greens. Peanut sauce was mixed in the vegetables. Fresh pecans and mangoes were served for dessert. While Sheldon and Suzette ate their Thai dinner they gazed around the Thai restaurant. There were miniature statuettes of Thai gods on shelves and vases with tropical plants and flowers arranged around the restaurant. Thai music was playing in the background. The restaurant walls were painted with bright orange, pink and yellow colors. Dangling plants hung from the ceiling.

Sheldon and Suzette especially enjoyed the peanut sauce and Thai wine, which came with the dinner. Their experience tasting Thai cuisine was a unique one. They enjoyed Thai cuisine and the friendly manners of the Thai servers.

The O'Connors dined out again the next weekend. They went to a Hindu-Indian restaurant. They made a reservation to secure a table for Friday night. Sheldon and Suzette arrived at the Hindu-Indian restaurant at

7:00 p.m. A Hindu-Indian hostess greeted them at the entrance and escorted them to a table in a good location in the largest room.

The O'Connors studied the menus to select their dinner. Sheldon selected their dinner. Sheldon selected roast duck with curried, rice, Indian vegetables and condiments and sliced vegetables, which were steamed and seasoned. Suzette selected curried lamb, curried rice and Indian curried vegetables. Coconut slices, banana slices and pineapple were served for dessert.

Sheldon and Suzette were served Pim's beer and Indian tea during their dinner. They tasted each dish of food, which were served in small bowls and dishes. The Hindu Indian restaurant was decorated with pictures and miniature statues of Hindu gods. A miniature water fountain flowed in a small manmade pond. The pond had lotus flowers on lily pods. Small fish were moving around in the pond. The water appeared blue against a painted, blue foundation.

Sheldon and Suzette enjoyed the unique setting in the Hindu Indian restaurant. Hindu music could be heard in the background. A fragrance of burning cedar incense permeated the restaurant. This special fragrance was refreshing and very pleasant.

After dinner the O'Connors enjoyed Hindu-Indian coffee. They left the restaurant at about 10 p.m. They felt full from dinner and went home well satisfied. Their unique experience at this restaurant was remembered. They remembered the spicy, delicious taste of the Indian cuisine. They planned to return again.

The next weekend was Chinese New Year in Chinatown in San Francisco. Sheldon and Suzette went to the Chinese New Year. A Chinese parade took place. There was a long, paper dragon, which was moved down the main street through Chinatown. Participants in the Chinese parade were dressed in colorful, traditional Chinese costumes. They marched down the street in a festive manner to celebrate Chinese New Year.

When the Chinese parade was over people prayed at Chinese pagodas in a nearby park. They prayed for another good year. Lanterns and Chinese decorations were dangling from shops and restaurants as well as business establishments in Chinatown.

After celebrating Chinese New Year the O'Connors stepped into one of the many Chinese restaurants to eat dinner. They walked upstairs to the restaurant. They were greeted by a Chinese hostess who escorted them to a table in the center of the restaurant. The O'Connors were handed menus.

Sheldon and Suzette selected various Chinese dishes from the menu. They ordered Peking duck, Chinese Chop Suey, Chinese Chow Mien, fried rice, egg-fu-young, wonton soup and shrimp. For dessert they had sliced oranges and fortune cookies. Chinese music was heard playing softly in the background.

This Chinese restaurant was elegantly decorated with Chinese tapestries, large pictures of Chinese gardens and Chinese landscapes. There were miniature statues of Goddess Kuan Yin and Confucius. Orange and red lanterns were dangling from the ceiling. The O'Connors had a magnificent view of San Francisco lit up at night to enjoy

All in all, Sheldon and Suzette had time and money to enjoy their dining out experiences.

FIFTY-THREE

KIDNAPPED

Kidnapping is a common experience especially in large, populated cities. Kidnappers force their victims to go into hiding. Sometimes the victims are tied up and kept in hidden places. Some kidnappers use guns or knives to scare their victims into compliance. They generally kidnap certain people knowing that they can collect a lot of money for ransom. Kidnappers know everyone wants their loved ones back. Some women kidnap someone elses child because these women want to have a child of their own to raise.

Priscilla Washburn was childless. She longed to have a child of her own. She applied at an adoption agency to acquire a child. However, there weren't enough children available. So Priscilla's request for a child was denied.

A year went by and Priscilla still wanted a child. She was unhappy and lonely. She continued to long for her own child. She was 35 now and she had been on her own for some time.

One day while Priscilla was walking in a large, central park she strolled along near trees and flowers at other people in this park. Priscilla observed families sitting on the grass and enjoying picnics. While other people were playing baseball, some children were playing on park equipment.

Priscilla noticed a girl toddler walking in the play area. This little girl had curly blonde haired, Caucasian and she appeared healthy. The child was dressed in a jumper and toddler shoes. Priscilla observed this little girl closely. She saw no adult around looking after the child.

The little girl sat down on the grass. She was playing with a small toy doll. Priscilla suddenly decided to grab the child from the park. No one attempted to stop Priscilla from kidnapping the little girl. Priscilla rushed out of the park with the toddler in her arms. She headed for her apartment, which was three blocks north of the park.

The little girl began to cry because she didn't know Priscilla. She wanted to be with her own mother. The little toddler was left with her older brother in the park while their mother went shopping at a grocery store. The older brother was playing kickball in the park. He wasn't watching his little sister well. He didn't notice that she was missing for at least fifteen minutes.

Johnny, her old brother, continued playing kickball. Finally, when he won the kickball game he walked over to where his younger sister was playing with younger children. Johnny noticed that his little sister, Peggy, was gone. He became worried and upset when she couldn't be found. So, he began asking other children if they had seen his little sister. A ten-year girl said, "I saw a woman take your sister out of the park." Johnny asked, "Which direction did she go in?" The ten-year-old girl pointed and said, "She went that way." She pointed north.

Johnny knew he was responsible for his little sister who was only 2 years old. He thanked the ten-year-old girl. Johnny headed north hoping to catch-up with Priscilla and his little sister, Peggy. He ran down the street calling for his sister. Priscilla and his little sister were nowhere in the distance. Johnny kept hunting for his sister.

Meanwhile, Priscilla returned to her apartment with Peggy. She brought Peggy into her rented dwelling, which was on the third floor. When she entered her apartment with Peggy in her arms she put her on the living room couch. Peggy was crying because she was in a strange place.

Priscilla tried to calm Peggy down. She went to the refrigerator and took out some ice cream in a bowl with a spoon. She gave Peggy the ice cream to eat. Peggy finally stopped crying. She began to eat the ice cream. It was strawberry flavored ice cream. Peggy enjoyed eating it all.

Priscilla spoke gently to Peggy. She told her that she would be taking care of her. She asked the little girl, "What is your name?" Peggy didn't answer. "So,"

Priscilla said, "I'm going to call you Zoë. That's a good name for you."

When Zoë had finished eating her ice cream, Priscilla brought some blankets into the living room. She had a rubber mattress in the closet, which she placed on the living room floor. She put a sheet on the mattress. Priscilla told Zoë to lie down on the mattress. Zoë came over to the mattress and sat on it. Priscilla laid her down on it. She covered her up with several blankets.

Zoë had calmed down because she enjoyed the ice cream. Priscilla stroked Zoë's hair. She massaged Zoë's back. Priscilla began singing to Zoë so she would go to sleep. After ten minutes Zoë fell asleep. She was tired from the day's activities.

Priscilla watched Zoë sleeping as she sat in a nearby chair. She knew she had kidnapped this little girl. She would be responsible for Zoë from now on. Next, she would buy Zoë some new clothes to wear. She would bathe Zoë in the morning. She finally had a child to take care of. Priscilla planned to keep Zoë to raise. She was happier now that she was not alone.

Johnny went to his home and told his mother that he couldn't find his little sister in the play area at the park. Johnny's mother was very upset. She scolded Johnny for not watching his little sister better. She called the police and reported that her daughter had been kidnapped. Johnny had told his mother that a woman took his little sister out of the park. Peggy's mother described her daughter to a policeman on the phone.

The police department sent policemen around to the area searching for a 2-year-old Caucasian toddler with curly blonde hair wearing a green jumper. Policemen searched around the park where she was kidnapped. They went up and down the streets in that neighborhood. They were not able to fine Peggy.

Years went by and Priscilla continued to raise Zoë, whose real name was Peggy. Zoë began to accept Priscilla as a mother substitute. She had no one else to care for her. Priscilla moved away from the area where she kidnapped Peggy. She took her to another city hundreds of miles away. Peggy, known as Zoë Washburn, went to school in Los Angeles, California. Pricilla created another birth certificate for the kidnapped child in order to change her identity. Her birth mother never was able to fine her daughter. She had to accept that her daughter had been kidnapped and possibly gone forever.

FIFTY-FOUR

PANDA EXPRESS DELIGHTS

Panda Express is a fast food buffet-type Chinese restaurant. Pan cooked vegetables and fried rice is served daily along with different, main courses. Main courses are sautéed chicken with string beans, sautéed chicken with asparagus, sautéed chicken with mushrooms and squash, beef with squash and mushrooms and spiced eggplant and squash.

Other side dishes are egg rolls, wontons, shrimp, sweet and sour pork. Fortune cookies and other cookies are available. Cold sodas such as Sprite, root beer, diet Coke, raspberry, and lemonade are available. Cold water is also available.

Panda Express has reasonable prices. Even a rice bowl topped with chicken or beef is available for only $2.00 and $3.00. Customers come into Panda Express and have a full course meal for a lower price. The people are attentive, clean and business-like. The décor is cheerful and bright. Pictures of panda bears can be seen. Pictures of China are displayed. Other artwork is also displayed.

Enjoy eating at Panda Express. The food is tasty, fresh and available when you walk in the door. Save some money and have a nutritious meal. Enjoy mango or raspberry iced or green tea with your meal.

FIFTY-FIVE

OVERCOMING GRIEF

A person can be overcome by grief. When loved ones die suddenly and gradually we feel sorrow and a deep sense of loss. How can a person learn to cope with grief? It takes being positive and detached to overcome strong, emotional ties to loved one that we miss and are separated from by death.

MaryAnn Jenkins was married for fifty-one years to her husband, Charles Jenkins. She was used to his companionship. She had spent most of her life with Charles. Suddenly, when Charles had turned 76 years old, he died in his sleep one night unexpectedly.

MaryAnn woke up the next morning expecting to say good morning to her husband. When she looked over at him in the double bed, he appeared very white and motionless. MaryAnn looked at him and said, "Good morning Charles." Charles did not answer her.

She touched Charles on the face. He didn't budge or open his eyes. She spoke to him repeatedly to wake him up. However, Charles didn't respond or wake up as he usually had done on previous mornings.

MaryAnn became alarmed and upset. She realized that Charles had passed away during the night. Mary Ann was 74 herself. She felt grief stricken when she found out that her husband was dead. MaryAnn had formed a deep attachment toward her husband over 51 years. She realized she was now alone and that she would have to accept the fact that she was a widow. She had hoped that Charles would have lived longer.

Funeral arrangements had to be made. MaryAnn called the minister of her Episcopal Church to make funeral arrangements. Charles' body was taken to the local mortuary to be prepared for the funeral services. Relatives and friends needed to be contacted about Charles' death and be invited to his funeral. Over fifty relatives and forty more friends were invited to attend the funeral.

MaryAnn continued to grieve for her husband. She felt lost without him at her side. She prepared meals for herself and ate alone in their two-bedroom home, which they had lived in for many years. MaryAnn kept crying and sobbing because of her husband's death.

The day of the funeral, a week later, MaryAnn dressed in black and wore a veil over her face. She went to the Episcopal Church where the funeral service was to take place. The minister read the eulogy about Charles Jenkins at the funeral. Vocal soloists sang several songs.

Floral arrangements were displayed on the casket and in the church. The minister read the eulogy about Charles life and accomplishments.

MaryAnn continued to cry and sob because she felt deeply grief-stricken about Charles' death. She reminisced about memories of her late husband. MaryAnn knew she would have to adjust to being a widow. She would have to accept her life without him.

Charles was invisible now to MaryAnn. He's spirit had gone on to the other side. MaryAnn was unable to speak to Charles ever again. She would never see Charles in his former body. She wasn't aware of his astral body, which existed on the astral plane because she as not psychic.

Over a period of time MaryAnn tried to accept Charles' death. However she kept remembering their life together. It took her some time to overcome her grief. Relatives and friends came to see MaryAnn trying to comfort her. Some relatives took her out for dinner. Friends took her to community activities. MaryAnn also attended the Episcopal Church on Sundays and she attended a Bible class once a week on Wednesday afternoon. This helped her to readjust to her life as a widow. She had to learn to become detached from her past with Charles. It was difficult for her to stop grieving because of his death. Charles would always have a special place in her heart with special memories.

FIFTY-SIX

PARANOIA REVEALED

Paranoia is caused from fear and lack of understanding about life experiences. A person may over react about how other people and even animals behave toward them. People who suffer from paranoia restrict themselves. They avoid challenges, risks and dangerous situations if they can.

Seanna Kellson grew up in a small town where everyone knows each other. Closed-minded, strict parents raised her. She became fearful of situations from other people and especially from risky experiences. She was told to stay in her family's yard. Seanna didn't play with other neighborhood children because she was told to stay in her parents' fenced in yard.

Seanna suffered from paranoia. She was easily afraid of insects such as spiders and bees. She was very frightened when she saw a snake slithering across the yard. She was afraid of other people, especially boys who behaved aggressively. Seanna was taught that spiders and snakes are all harmful. This is why Seanna reacted strongly with fear and worry.

Sometimes Seanna stayed awake all night. She couldn't sleep because she was afraid of the dark. She kept a light on all night. Sometimes she had nightmares when she fell asleep. She would wake up screaming and shaking with fear. She would lie in her bed and continue to think about her nightmares.

As Seanna continued to grow up she continued to suffer from paranoia. She was afraid to express herself in school during class discussions, question and answer times. Seanna was shy and withdrawn because she had not learned to open up and express herself freely. Paranoia was revealed when Seanna became anxious and fearful. She reacted strongly to loud unexpected sounds and movements.

Would Seanna be able to overcome her fears and anxieties, which she had acquired? She was even afraid to be a passenger in a car, bus or train. She had never been in an airplane. She was afraid of heights.

When Seanna was 18 she graduated from high school. She was still shy and experiencing paranoia. Her family didn't have enough money so she could receive psychiatric guidance. One day she was walking downtown. She happened to come to a Scientology Center. She stopped at the doorway. She was curious about what Scientology meant.

Someone in the Scientology Center noticed Seanna standing at the door. Sharon, who was a Scientologist, came over to the door to greet Seanna. She invited her into the Scientology Center. So, Seanna walked in and looked around. She noticed people sitting at e-meters. Auditors were interviewing them. Sharon showed Seanna around. She told Seanna what Scientology signified. She explained how people were cured of lower emotions such as fear, hate, greed, malice and violence by measuring their emotions on an e-meter.

Seanna was encouraged to sit near an e-meter. An auditor known as Joshua interviewed her. Joshua asked Seanna questions about her fears and worries. Seanna was reluctant to reveal her feelings about her life. Joshua realized that Seanna was shy and that she wasn't used to expressing her thoughts about what she felt. He had experience in how to help shy, frightened individuals to open up to reveal their feelings.

Joshua asked Seanna to tell him what she was afraid of. She finally responded. Seanna said, "I don't liked big, black spiders." She continued, "Spiders bite!" Seanna looked at Joshua. She replied, "No, but my parents have told me to stay away from spiders because they kill people." Joshua asked, "Have you witnessed anyone dying from spider bites?" Seanna stared at Joshua. She answered, "No."

Joshua said, "You don't need to be afraid of spiders. You should avoid Black Widows and other poisonous kinds of spiders. However, garden spiders in general won't harm you. Put your hand on this e-meter." Seanna put her hand on the e-meter. It measured her emotion. It measured fear. Seanna still was afraid of spiders. She had a strong feeling about spiders. It would take more interviews to overcome her reaction to spiders.

Sharon and Joshua encouraged Seanna to come back to the Scientology Center. So, Seanna began attending the Scientology Center several days a week. She was charged very little money to experience interviewers who audits her. Gradually, Seanna began to overcome her fears, inhibitions and anxieties as she revealed how and why she had felt negative emotions.

Seanna became a more adjusted person once she released her fears and worries. Her emotions were measured on an e-meter. In time, her emotions were neutralized. Seanna opened up and was able to express herself much better. She experienced clearness and she developed a more positive outlook and attitude about life. She became a volunteer auditor at the Scientology Center to help newcomers.

FIFTY-SEVEN

SEEK PEACE OF MIND

Seek peace of mind by calming your outer mind. Overcome your lower emotions of resentment, dislike, hatred, jealousy, avarice and malice. Lower emotions tend to create barriers and restrictions in our minds. We need to realize how to control our lower emotions.

Meditation is a way to calm your lower emotions. Silence your mind to control unnecessary feelings and reactions about important situations and negative experiences. Find a quiet place to meditate. You can meditate in your bedroom or under a tree. You can meditate on the beach near the ocean or in a garden.

Beautiful surroundings add to a peaceful environment. A quiet location may help you calm down in order to seek peace. Peaceful, positive thoughts help uplift one's mind and to release negative thoughts.

Gautama Buddha, Krishna, Jesus, Gandhi, Yogananda and others had learned how to control their emotions. They had learned to go within seeking inner peace and oneness with God. They had learned to become One with their I AM Presence. As a result, they had control over lower emotions.

Most people can acquire peace of mind. Some individuals practice yoga, which helps them develop physical and mental control and positive concentration. Peace of mind is possible. Each person should learn to seek inner peace and harmony on a daily basis.

FIFTY-EIGHT

FINGER PRINTS TELL

Fingerprints are taken today. Everyone is fingerprinted so they can be identified legally with electronic image files at the courthouses and police stations. Fingerprints are kept on birth certificates today.

Each fingerprint is unique to one individual. The lines in one's fingers are designed differently. A person can be easily identified immediately by his or her fingerprints on record from the F.B I. Information Bureau.

Fingerprints were not used and thought of as a way to identify a person until 75 to 85 years ago. No one noticed or discovered that fingerprints were unique to every human being throughout the Earth.

Fingerprints tell us that we are all different from one another in terms of our fingerprints. Without fingerprints it is very difficult to prove who vandalized or murdered someone. Fingerprints can be found at most crime scenes.

Policemen collect fingerprints at crime scenes. Fingerprints are able to be used to prove who committed certain crimes. Fingerprints are very useful in discovering who caused a crime. On the other hand, they are used by criminal investigating bodies to also exclude potential suspects from a criminal case. Past long-term criminals that were falsely accused and locked up based on evidence then are being freed from prison do to the ability of more sophisticated, lab work, technique investigators who found decisive fingerprints that excluded them as suspects. Many already incarcerated prisoners were the perpetrators of some of these crimes.

Even when gloves are worn by perpetrators, sometimes fingerprints can still be detected and detected with special instruments. Fingerprints tell a lot about one's DNA.

FIFTY-NINE

HOW TO BE LIKED BY OTHERS

We all want to be liked by others. We want to be respected and appreciated by our parents, brothers and sisters, other relatives, friends and acquaintances. We try to please others. We even try to impress others so they will like us. We try to be vivacious, pleasant and likeable.

Julie Williams was 16 years old. She wanted to be popular. She joined the cheerleaders at her high school. Julie became the leader of the cheerleaders. She dressed in a colorful, cheerleader outfit with a short skirt to draw attention.

Cheerleaders practiced after school to prepare for football and basketball games. There were 20 cheerleaders. They used pom-poms, which they lifted up in the air. They moved pom-poms around in all different directions as they choreographed their cheerleading routines for the student body during sports and special school events.

Cheerleaders became well known for their performances before school spectators at different school activities. They also were popular with the basketball and football players who asked them out for dates.

Julie wanted to date Dale Rommel, who was one of the best football players at her high school. Julie had long, slender, legs, which gracefully carried her about. Her legs were attractive. Dale was attracted to Julie. She responded to him because she liked him.

Dale picked Julie up at her parents' home on Saturday night at 7 p.m. Julie was dressed in a stylish pantsuit. Her hair was styled with curls, which softened her face. She wore lipstick and eyelash darkener to make her eyes stand out.

Julie wanted to be attractive so Dale would desire to be with her. There were other attractive, high school girls he could go out on dates with. Yet, he chose Julie to date. Dale took Julie to dinner and then to a movie downtown. They had a good time. Dale held Julie's hand in the theater. They saw a recent film about Paradise Island.

Dale especially enjoyed the film about Paradise Island. He told Julie that he wished he could go to Hawaii for a vacation. His parents were planning to go to Hawaii someday for two weeks to see all four, major islands. Dale told Julie he hoped she could join his parents and himself next summer when they were going to Hawaii.

Julie and Dale became romantically involved more and more. Julie fell in love with Dale. He was tall, well built with dark hair and brown eyes. Dale dressed well and many high school girls were attracted to him.

Dale continued to date Julie. He ignored other high school girls wanting to date him because he wanted to be exclusive with Julie. Julie was so glad that Dale cared about her so much.

Julie became one of the most popular girls at high school. She was admired and respected for her accomplishments at high school. She was vivacious, cheerful and interesting as a person to know. Even if she was attractive she was not stuck up. She didn't act like she was better than anyone else. She was genuinely warm and friendly toward everyone. She graduated from high school with honors a few years later.

Dale's parents took Julie and Dale to Hawaii during the summer for two weeks. They toured the four major islands. They went to Oahu where they enjoyed the Polynesian Cultural Center. They went walking on Waikiki Beach and they went swimming.

A highlight of the trip was the zoo at Waikiki. Julie and Dale fed the monkeys and elephants. They attended some Hawaiian shows and toured the island of Oahu, Maui, the big island and Kauai. The beaches were magnificent. The ocean was turquoise-blue. The weather was pleasant. Hawaiians were friendly to Julie and Dale and his parents. They all had a wonderful time. They hoped they could come back to Hawaii someday.

Best of all, Julie felt good because she was liked as well as loved for herself. She was accepted by her peers, which made a difference to her. She developed self-esteem.

SIXTY

SHOCKING NEWS

Shocking news is revealed on television, radio, in newspapers and magazines. We hear about people killed in airplane crashes, in skiing and automobile accidents and on mountain climbing expeditions. We hear about innocent civilians killed during wars, dangerous floods and during bomb tests.

When loved ones have been suddenly killed in an accident of some kind, we feel devastated and grief-stricken. We have to forgive these tragedies and mishaps. It takes time to overcome the shocking news. We must eventually become detached in order to accept the unpleasant news.

Everyday people may encounter dangers, unexpected diseases and injuries such as broken bones, fractures, bruises and cuts. People are taken to the emergency ward in ambulances because of sudden or prolonged illness or accidents. Some victims do not recover once they become ill or are in an accident. They must cope with their illnesses and accidents.

Shocking news carries emotional stress, sadness and anxiety. We must learn to endure and forgive sudden, unexpected and shocking news. There are many accidents and illnesses on the Earth. Changing weather may cause damaging hurricanes, typhoons and cyclones. Homes and public buildings and electrical wires may be suddenly destroyed. People become homeless suddenly.

Fires spread suddenly and unexpectedly, which cause a lot of damage to forests, landscapes in general and to homes and other buildings. It may take many days and nights to put out fires. People hear the shocking news about devastating fires.

We must be on the lookout at all times and hope we will remain safe and healthy.

SIXTY-ONE

GLAMOUR ISN'T THAT IMPORTANT

In America, a Western society, women and men focus on being glamorous. Women and men go on strict diets to maintain sliminess. Being slim has been the fashion for sometime.

Women dress up in high fashion, fancy clothes and wear attractive hairstyles. They put on eye makeup, skin creams and colorful lipsticks. Women cover skin blemishes and wrinkles with makeup in order to appear more glamorous. Women want to impress men by coloring their hair different colors. They try different hairdos that they think are attractive.

Glamour is focused on especially in high society. Women try to allure men with their beauty and grooming. They have their fingernails and toenails shaped and stylishly paint them in designs to appear more glamorous and eye appealing. Often competition is fierce with other women for men's admiration hoping to find that special someone in their life. Women like to wear attractive jewelry to look their best.

However, glamour should not be so important. The kind of person you become is far more important. You can be neat, clean and wear simple clothes. Quite often men relax more around women who do not try to be glamorous. A man wants a woman who is faithful and who he can trust. She doesn't have to be too glamorous to be appreciated.

Men who seek glamorous women may be disappointed when these glamorous women are unfaithful as well as vain. Quite often a beautiful woman is spoiled because of the attention she receives from many men. While a $45.00 fingernail job for long decorated nails may be impressive for some, it isn't practical unless they are in a sales presentation business where their hands are in constant full view demonstrations. For most mothers and husbands trimmed and clean fingernail are more desirable for health reasons and every day living purposes. Long nails tend to snag many kinds of clothing materials. If your profession requires typing, use of tools or work gloves including home chores simple manicured nails fare much better.

So, glamour should not be so important. Character and pleasant behavior and positive attitudes are for more valuable as well as appreciated. Men are basically simple to please. Most men want to be recognized for being the man of the house, food, a loving spouse, and win an occasional family discussion. In other words, overdoing make up and hairdos is unnecessary. Just be your own sweet self and your honey will worship the ground you walk on. Quite often a beautiful woman is spoiled because of the attention she receives from many men. No spouse would appreciate that competition.

SIXTY-TWO

ILLUSIONS MAY FOOL YOU

Illusions may fool us. We see an apparition, which appears to be real or we see a passing shadow, which creates images. Our minds may play tricks on us especially when we fall asleep and dream. We wake up and feel our illusions are real.

Illusions may occur frequently. We have many imaginary thoughts. We create thoughts and recall many memories. Our memories may still be vivid in our minds. However, we may add new thoughts and attitudes to reflect on our memories of the past.

Girls often imagine what it is like to go on dates with boys. Women, who are single, imagine being with men. They hope to attract the right man and get married. Girls tend to dream about the perfect man to come a long. The only reason why girls and boys should be dating is to determine if they're going to be a good match for them. They make up illusions about a man they want to meet.

A person creates illusions constantly in their regular thought process. Many imaginary thoughts occur in one's stream of consciousness. Around 80% of one's thoughts are not factual. We need to learn to concentrate on how to think accurately based on real happenings and factual information. Right action and right concentration should be our goals.

Illusions often fool people. We must realize what is happening around us. We need to face reality. If a person constantly hallucinates, he or she is not facing life directly. Illusions have their place. However, real experiences are more valid. Illusions should be controlled. When we face realities we are able to adjust better and accept our lives better.

SIXTY-THREE

A NORMAL LIFE

We are told from birth on what is normal as well as what is not good behavior. Normal behavior is acceptable behavior.

When a baby cries because it is wet and uncomfortable this is considered normal. If a baby constantly cries and it is clean and dry and has eaten enough this is considered abnormal. The baby is crying for some unknown reason.

Children are taught ways to learn about home life, about what foods to eat and how to act in an acceptable manner. If a child eats unacceptable foods such as dirt, poisonous spiders or unclean garbage, the parents are in charge and responsible for their life. Therefore, they need to be taught right from wrong.

It is normal for children to play games and to experience spontaneous, imaginary play time. Children who become uninvolved and stay by themselves are behaving abnormally.

We are taught what is right and what is wrong. Normal behavior is right action with the right association. We are told there are average or normal grades in the grading system in school. Below average grades are not passing grades.

Normal behavior is learned step-by-step, day-by-day, and month-to-month over a period of years. Parent and teachers clarify what is proper, acceptable behavior. Children who do not follow certain acceptable behavioral patterns are considered misbehaved. They may be labeled as abnormal. Normal behavior is the acceptable way

SIXTY-FOUR

NEW BEGINNINGS

New beginnings are necessary in everyone's' life. We all need a fresh start from time to time. A child begins school in kindergarten when he or she is 5 ½ years old. At 5 ½ years old a child has a lot to learn as beginners.

After eighth grade a teenager begins high school. This new beginning is a new start in higher education. High school freshmen begin with more advanced curriculum. They continue to learn more about English, Mathematics, Science, Social Studies, Biology, Calculus, Physics, Physical Education, Music, Art and Wood Craft, etc.

New cycles are new beginnings. Manvantaras last for 432,000,000 years. The next Manvantara is thousands of years in the future during a Manvantara. Each lifetime gives us a chance and a new beginning to experiences life on Earth. During each incarnation a soul can grow and develop spiritually, mentally and physically. Some souls evolve faster than others. Souls who evolve and develop mastery are able to become avatars known as world teachers. The world teachers can serve humanity with their wisdom and enlightenment.

New beginnings occur within our physical cells. Our body cells reproduce constantly. In seven years we have new skin. Our body organs are regenerated and restored so we can survive. Every new breath keeps us alive.

There is a beginning as well as ending to books, articles, stories, poems and reports, etc. A speech has a beginning and ending. A song or instrumental piece has a beginning and ending. Creations such as human beings, plants and animals are born and they eventually die. Every physical life form has a certain life cycle that begins and ends.

We need new beginnings in order to improve our lives and to expand our awareness. Self-growth and personal development are part of spiritual, physical and mental development. The purpose of life is to learn about many experiences and to evolve into maturity.

SIXTY-FIVE

SPARKLING PERSONALITIES

Some individuals have a lot of charisma and personal charm. These individuals sparkle and radiate with light. Their eyes shine brightly and they smile with warmth. Usually individuals with sparkling personalities are readily noticed and liked by other people. They tend to be popular and well liked.

Sheila Parsons had a sparkling personality. She became a beautician when she was twenty years old. She met many men, women and children who she had as customers. Sheila was very pleasant and charming to her customers. She joked and laughed a lot around them.

Customers felt comfortable around Sheila because she helped them to relax. She was an excellent beautician. She was able to cut hair into a variety of styles. She curled hair with rollers and curling irons. Each hairstyle she combed out looked attractive and modern.

Sheila visited with her clients. She became familiar with most of her clients. She learned a lot about some of her clients. Sheila had a full daily schedule booked with one client after the next. Sheila was bubbly and vivacious. So, she was well liked by her clients. She was a successful beautician.

Melinda Jones was an elementary school teacher. She had a sparkling personality. She expressed herself well in her classroom. She taught fourth grade in a town where she lived in Arroyo Grande, California. Melinda had been teaching for twelve years.

Melinda Jones was well liked by her students. She expressed herself very well and she had very good eye contact. Her eyes lit up when she spoke to her students.

Mrs. Jones organized Social Studies and Science committees in her classroom. Students worked in groups to present topics with research and visual materials. Sheila helped her students learn to communicate effectively in groups. A leader, co-leader and resource helpers were assigned to specific roles and responsibilities in each committee.

Sheila Jones was able to communicate will with many students, her friends, relatives and even acquaintances because she was an open and well rounded person. She enjoyed communicating with others. She also had many hobbies such as reading, tennis, golf, community clubs and dancing. She enjoyed listening to a wide variety of music. She had learned to play the piano, organ and guitar. She was versatile in many things. She was well educated and she had read many books. Most of all, she had a sparkling personality.

SIXTY-SIX

ICELAND WONDERLAND

Iceland is an island of fire and ice. One third of Iceland is covered in ice. However, there is volcanic activity, natural hot springs and geysers. Iceland is isolated. Yet, it has become a more technologically and socially advanced nations in the world.

The Vikings were the first to settle in Iceland. The early settlers organized themselves into a commonwealth governed by the first parliament in Northern Europe. Icelanders depend on fishing and fish processing economically. Geothermal and hydro-electrical energy is used in Iceland.

Today, Iceland is independent and nationalistic. Icelanders have maintained their language, customs and heritage. Iceland's current high standards of living and learning are an example of progressive living.

Iceland is an island in the North Atlantic midway between America and continental Europe. It is south of the Arctic Circle on the same latitude as Fairbanks, Alaska. It is warmed by the flow of the Gulf Stream. Iceland is about the size of Ohio in the U.S.A.

Much of Iceland is uninhabitable. Most of the interior is covered by permanent ice or lava or is a high plateau on which little grows. Fishing communities are near the sea. Iceland is mountainous with volcanic activity. Iceland is full of hot springs and rivers, which often flow down spectacular waterfalls on their way to the sea.

Iceland is a country of breathtaking, unspoiled, natural beauty. The uninhabited land is primarily in the interior. Half of this is desert plateau above 1,500 feet where little grows. Eleven percent of Iceland is covered with glaciers. Iceland's largest glacier, Vatnajokull, is the largest ice cap in Europe. It covers 3,240 square miles, which is almost half the area of New Jersey. At some places the ice of this glacier is over 3,000 feet thick.

Inhabited Iceland is at the perimeter of this island. There is a single highway that circles the island. Over half the population lives in a small part of the southwest, centering on Reykjavik. Extending southwest from Reykjavik is a peninsula of inhospitable lava exposed to the North Atlantic on, which is located the U.S. Marine Airbase of Keflavik and the international airport. Farther south and east of Rekjavik is the best farmland in Iceland.

Situated inland is the largest lake Thingvallavatn, which covers 32 square miles. On its shore is Thingvellir, the site of the first Icelandic parliament. Also, found here are the geysers at Geyser. Off the south coast is Westmann, Iceland, which is harsh, volcanic islands that include Surtsey, newly formed by a volcanic eruption in 1963. On the mainland, in the southeast, the glacier Vatnajokull extends almost to the sea. Along the southern coast are numerous sandur, wasteland of black sand and volcanic debris deposited by the glacial run-offs, along with innumerable rivers.

Iceland's second largest city, Akureyri, is at the head of a fjord in the north center of the island east of the north center of this island. East of this city is Myvatn, know as Midge Lake, in a fertile valley close to fields of lava. Grimsey, a small island off the north coast, is the only part of Iceland to extend into the Arctic Circle.

The northwest is covered with deep fjords and steep mountains and is inhabited mostly by fishing communities. Hornstrandir has less population since the first half of the 20th century. It has been designated as a nature reserve because thousands of birds that nest on the cliffs.

Iceland is situated at the point where two tectonic plates, vast landmasses that float on the Earth's central magma, are parting. The plate supporting North America is pulling away from that one supporting Europe and Africa. The movement of the plates results in earthquakes and volcanic eruptions. The gap is filled with lava. Iceland is continuing to grow at least one inch a year.

Icelanders have used energy contained in geological, hot spots. Hot water is piped to provide heated swimming pools in most Icelandic communities. More advanced technologies are used to heat most buildings with geothermal energy piped in from these "hotspots."

The climate of Iceland is moderate. The warming effect of the Gulf Stream keeps temperatures in Reykjavik from falling much below freezing. In January the temperature is 31°F. Summers are not hot. It is usually 52° in July in Iceland. Reykjavik has considerable rain. There is less rain and clouds on other parts of Iceland.

Snow falls at least 100 days a year in the northwest portion of Iceland. The southeast of Iceland averages about 40 snowy days per year. Strong winds are common throughout Iceland. In the sandur and some area of the interior, dust storms make travel very difficult.

The length of a day varies greatly with the time of year. In summer, Iceland is a land of midnight sun. In winter, night never ends. The only land mammal in Iceland is the arctic fox. Polar bears are rare visitors to Iceland. A variety of rodents including rats and mice live in Iceland. Reindeer came from Norway in the 18th Century. They roam wild in the eastern portion of the country. Harbor seals and gray seals breed on the coast. Walruses are rare. Whales were once common. However, hunters have made them less available. The killer whale, or Orcas, is now the most common. There are occasional sightings of sperm whales, fin whales, humpback and mink whales exist near Iceland.

Iceland is a bird watcher's paradise. About 70 species of birds breed here, while another 230 species have been sited. Iceland birds include the gyrfalcon, a large falcon found only in Iceland, the white-tailed eagle, and the ptarmigan. A species of grouse are hunted by both gyrfalcons and humans. There are many species of ducks, including elder ducks, the sea base ducks whose feathers are valued for their warmth and softness in the making of eiderdown. There are many colonies of sea birds, including gannets, fulmar, kittiwakes, guillemots and many more. There are three species of birds, the great aul, which is a large, flightless seabird that is now extinct; puffins are Iceland's most common birds with a population of 8 to 10 million. These small birds catch fish at sea and make nests by digging burrows into sea cliffs in huge communities. Icelanders hunt them for food by using puffin-catchers.

Arctic terns nest extensively throughout Iceland. These birds migrate each winter from Antarctica, 10,000 miles away. These birds dive-bomb intruders to protect their nests and young. Their eggs must be protected. Kria is another name for the Arctic tern.

Reykjavik is the largest city in Iceland consisting of 187,263 people as of 2006. It is a clean, modern city with a harbor and airport, which handles domestic flights. The international airport is located in Keflavik, south of Reykjavik. Reykjavik is the cultural center of Iceland. There is a symphony orchestra, theater, museum and library as well as hotels and restaurants. It is the site of the university, the parliament and a major cathedral.

Reykjavik is the principal commercial and industrial center of Iceland. The region was first settled around 870 A.D. In 1918 Reykjavik became the capitol of Iceland.

Residential homes in Reykjavik are generally built of concrete and brightly colored roofs. This city attracts tourists.

Akureyri is the second largest city. Akureyri is a small town by European standards with a population of only 16,736. Akureyri was established in 1786. It is located in the middle of the north coast at the sheltered end of long fjord. It is a major fishing harbor and is also the center for tourism in the northern half of the country.

Isafjordour, with a population of 2,777, is the major town on the Vestfirdhir, the western fjords peninsula. It is surrounded by steep mountains. This picturesque, small town is centered on its harbor with fishing and fish processing as the city's major economic activities.

Icelanders have a strong sense of tradition. During festivals, Icelanders sample traditional foods. Some people wear traditional dress during festivals—like Independence Day. Icelanders typically dress more like Americans and Europeans today.

Traditional national costumes have been revived by the Reykjavik Folk Dancing Society and as part of the Independence Day festivities. Women's traditional dress consists of a black skirt of homespun clothe and a black knitted cardigan with a high neckline, long sleeves and a slight opening above the breast to give a view of a white shirt underneath. Fancy dresses are made of linen, velvet and silk. Such a dress is completed with a silk neckerchief like a cravat and a waist belt. Most striking of all is the headwear, either a knitted cap with a tassel or a tall, white cascading headdress. The men's traditional dress consists of a dark-colored tunic and breeches tucked into long socks. Men also wear cravat-like neckerchiefs and distinctive headgear, long, conical, woolen caps.

Icelanders are dedicated workers and consumers. They have a very strong work ethic. Children, who are 12 years of age, work during the summer. Many adults hold two jobs. Icelanders work a longer week than most people in other industrialized nations. Money must be earned to pay for food, clothes, traveling and cultural events.

Long dark winters affect Icelanders. They may go to parties and drink as well as listen to music, to read and write. People must have worthwhile activities to keep them busy during much longer days.

Icelanders live in a stark but beautiful setting where they have to struggle against the natural elements of earthquakes and glaciers, rough seas and swollen rivers, cold weather and long periods of darkness during winter months. Above all, people there have a high standard of living. There is enough employment for all.

Icelanders' society is small and cohesive, which means that it lacks diversity and can seem oppressively normal. This also helps it to be relatively classless and crimeless. Icelandic culture mythologizes the independent—spirited individual; but Icelanders also value family and community.

Icelanders have very good healthcare. The infant mortality rate is one of the lowest in the world. The Iceland population is growing every year. Child-rearing duties are given to mothers because fathers are generally working very longer hours. Day care centers are kept busy because mothers must work to provide enough money to pay for moderate living expenses.

Students in school are required to take swimming. Danish is taught from the fourth grade on. English is taught from sixth grade on. Children are not divided by abilities at this level of schooling. Students participate in a range of sports with handball and soccer being the two most popular. Horseback riding is popular for boy and girls.

At the end of the ninth grade a standardized test along with the school's record of assessment is used to select what institutions a young Icelander should go to next. Students go to secondary or comprehensive school for four years (ages 16 to 19) or to vocational school. Some students leave school altogether at 16. These people will fill the less skilled jobs.

Iceland has five universities, which are the University of Iceland in Reykjavik, the University of Akureyri, the Iceland University of Education, the Reykjavik University, and the Technical College of Iceland. They are all state-funded and tuition free.

Icelanders are family minded. They may not marry before having children. They go camping and skiing. Swimming is a popular sport. There are well heated outside pools to swim in. Women live usually to be 82 years of age. Men usually live to be 79 years of age. Ninety five percent of Icelanders are Lutherans. A portion of Icelanders' taxes goes to support church activities. Some Icelanders believe in ghosts and trolls. Icelanders have a richness of medieval, prose literature.

Iceland is a wonderland for tourists to enjoy. Hot springs, a variety of birds, fjords and swimming pools exist in Iceland. Plan to visit Iceland during summertime.

SIXTY-SEVEN

KNOW YOURSELF

Know yourself. You will be able to be fulfilled. You can experience higher consciousness. Expand your mind and become aware and enlightenment. Enlightenment will awaken you to truth and wisdom. With wisdom and higher knowledge you will be inspired and uplifted. Higher knowledge can help you understand the cosmic plan and creations.

Know yourself so you can become One with God. God consciousness should be your goal. The purpose of life is so we can grow and evolve to know God. Step-by-step our inner self can emerge and unfold.

We exist in seven planes. These planes are the I Am Presence, Christ Self, Soul Presence, mental body, emotional body, astral body and physical body. We need to understand our seven bodies and planes to know ourselves. Awareness of our I Am Presence, Christ

Self and Soul Presence is important so we can mature spiritually.